The Body in Action

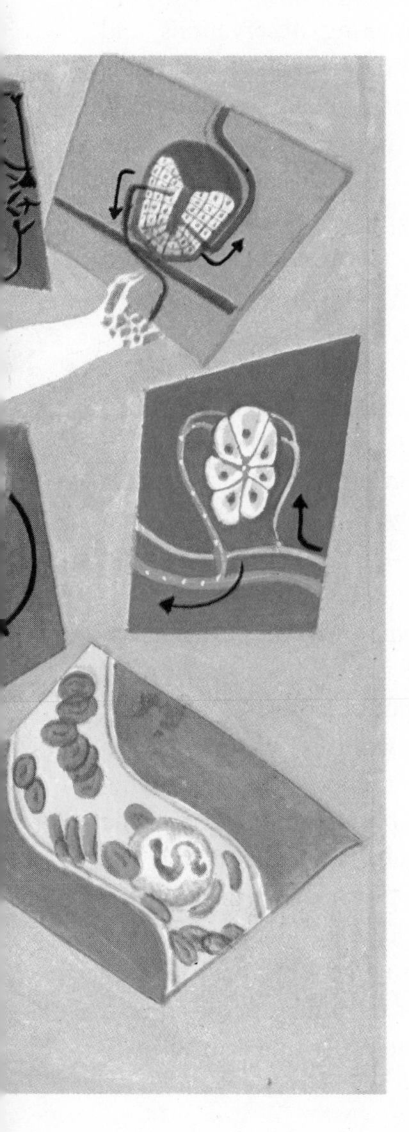

THE PARTS OF THE BODY AND HOW THEY WORK

based on The Human Body

by Mitchell Wilson

text especially adapted

by Ann Reit

illustrated

by Cornelius De Witt

GOLDEN PRESS NEW YORK

Designed and produced by Artists and Writers Press, Inc. Printed in the U.S.A. by Western Printing and Lithographing Company. Published by Golden Press, Inc., New York. Published simultaneously in Canada by The Musson Book Company, Ltd., Toronto.

Library of Congress Catalog Card Number: 62-13730

Introduction

Almost nothing, it seems, could be more important to man than the human body. Yet thousands and thousands of years passed before man really learned much about this part of himself.

Among the ancients, health was something given by the gods. The few real facts that were known were badly mixed up with superstition.

The first ancient thinker to fight free from superstition was a Greek of the fifth century B.C., Hippocrates. Much like a modern scientist, he observed the human body carefully, wrote down what he saw, and drew conclusions from his observations.

But men like Hippocrates are few. After the Golden Age of Greece, scientific thinking became rare. For nearly two thousand years, new ideas and the questioning of old ones were discouraged by religious authorities. Testing and experimenting were not proper for men of learning. Scholars concentrated on problems of religion, and they inherited their ideas from the past.

At the close of the middle ages, however, the world was changing. Merchants were traveling more widely. Thoughtful people were becoming restless and impatient with old ideas. Columbus and his voyages were just one sign of the times.

It was just about fifty years after Columbus discovered America that an Italian thinker, Vesalius, discovered the human body. Vesalius was one of those people who were taking a fresh inquiring look at the world—asking questions of the kind that mean scientific progress. Vesalius went much further than Hippocrates in making observations and setting up standards of study for others to follow. When he had the opportunity, he performed dissections on dead bodies to learn about their insides. Fine illustrations of the body drawn by an artist under his direction made a great impression, and thousands of people learned from them.

It is hard to believe that most of the facts of human anatomy known today by high school students were unknown only four hundred years ago. We have come a long way since then. The road of learning has been hard and slow, and any doctor will be quick to say that much is still unknown. But everyone today can have a clear understanding of the more important parts of the body and how they work.

Why is that important? The living body is probably the greatest scientific wonder of the world, and so it is the perfect subject with which to begin the study of science. Knowledge of the body helps to keep us healthy. And for any young person planning to become a doctor or a nurse, the study of the body is a first step.

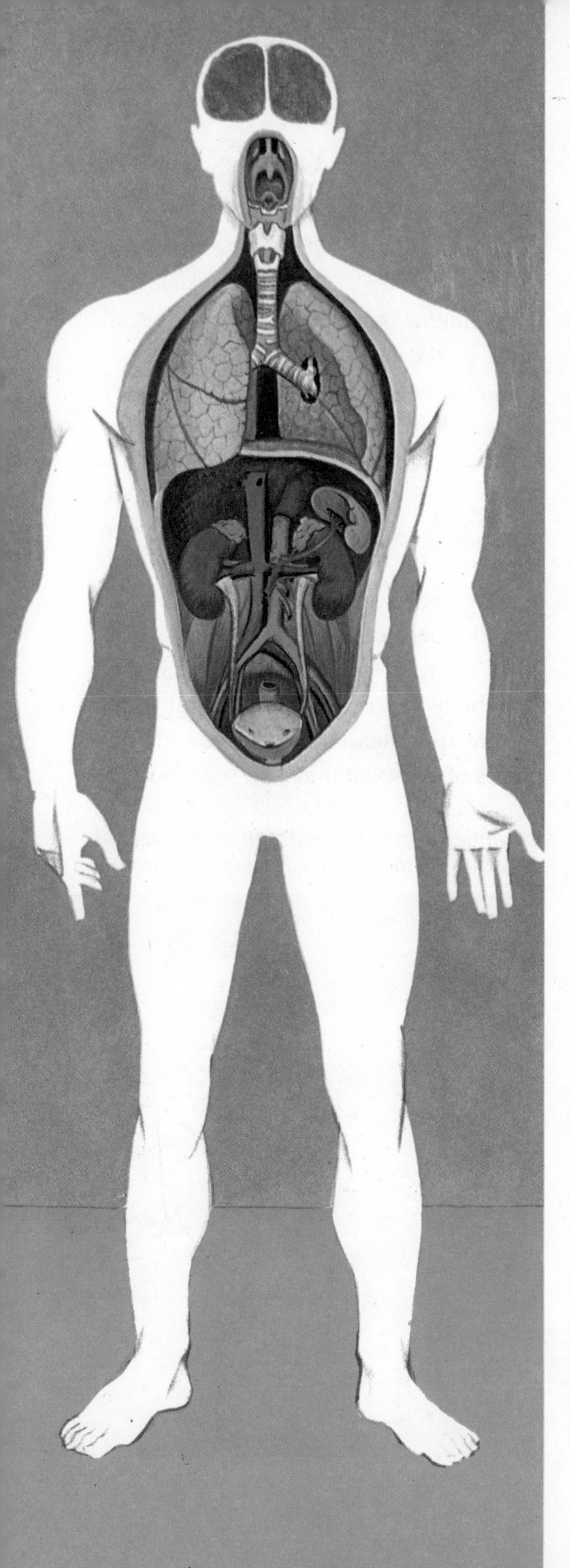

The Wonder of Life

No other form of life is as marvelous as the human body. No other form is as complex, nor can any do so many things. Every part of the body is alive, and virtually every part works to keep the whole body alive.

Any living thing feeds itself and must have food to stay alive. Some animals eat leaves, berries, or grass; others need meat. Trees and other plants take in food through roots in the ground.

All species of living things are able to create offspring almost in their own likeness. The tiny creatures of the water create new minute creatures like themselves. Trees drop seeds that grow to become new trees. Hens have baby chicks. Human beings give birth to children. This is called reproduction.

Only living creatures, then, can feed and reproduce. Even the smallest, simplest form of life feeds and reproduces. This simplest form of life is called a one-celled organism.

Like all complicated creatures, the human being is actually made up of billions of single cells, of which there are many kinds. The final human being is, of course, very different from any of the single cells that help make him up. There is no single-celled creature in the world that can laugh, sing, dance, read, know what joy feels like, or how it is to be sad, or the fun of learning something new.

Cells

The cell is the smallest unit of life. Life began many millions of years ago in the sea, and probably as a result of this origin, the cell is made up largely of liquid. The cell can be thought of as a very tiny globe with a liquid center and a thin, protective cover—called a membrane—enclosing it. The entire life of the cell is regulated by the membrane. All the nourishment the cell receives filters into it through the membrane, and the cell's waste products filter out through it. If the membrane is damaged or destroyed, the cell dies.

The membrane encloses the cell's fluid, and in this fluid is suspended a still smaller droplet which is enclosed by another membrane. Like the meat inside a nut, this is the most important part of the cell and is called the nucleus, from the Latin word for the kernel, or inside part, of a nut. The nucleus itself could be called a cell except that it cannot live without the cell fluid around it. In the nucleus lie all the materials that are used by the cell to reproduce itself. Digestion of food takes place in the cell fluid, and there also the cell stores up extra food that it will use at a later time.

Different kinds of cells do special jobs in the body. Gland cells produce and give out special juices that the body needs. For example, the cells of the sweat glands secrete a fluid that no other kind of cell can make. Muscle cells are so formed that they can tighten and relax, and so move the various parts of the body. Nerve cells are the only cells in the body that can pass along messages from the parts of the body to the brain or spinal cord. There are at least a half-dozen different types of cells that make up the blood.

Simple organisms feed and reproduce. A hydra's tentacles wave food into its mouth.

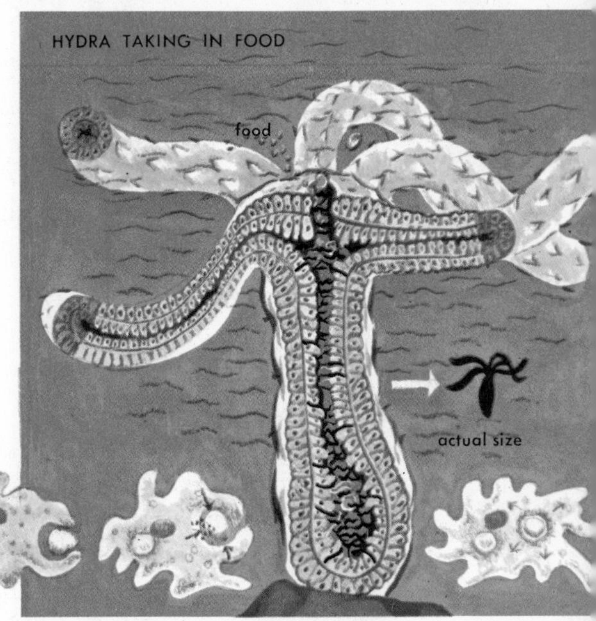

The cells are life's building blocks. Just as bridges, houses, and machines are all made up of small, simple parts, so all living things—from the one-celled ameoba to the human body—are made up of cells.

When a large number of the same kind of cells are found together, they are said to form tissue. In the body there are six kinds of tissue.

The first kind is covering tissue. Examples of this are the skin and the covering of the inside of the mouth, and the digestive organs.

A second kind is connective tissue. It binds muscles together, forms the capsules around joints, anchors organs in place, and forms a loose supporting network under the skin. The blood is a third kind of tissue. Muscle tissue is the fourth, nervous tissue the fifth, and glandular tissue the sixth.

Nervous tissue is different from all the others because it is the only kind of tissue that cannot heal itself by growing new nerve cells. Damaged skin, for example, is healed when the skin cells reproduce and create new skin cells to take the place of those that were destroyed. The same is true of muscle cells. Bone tissue can heal, and even blood renews itself.

A group of different tissues working together to do a special job forms a mass called an organ. An eye is an organ, as are the brain, the heart, the liver, and many other parts of the body.

A group of organs that work together is called a system. For example, the mouth, the stomach, and the intestines are organs that work together for the handling of food. They make up part of the digestive system.

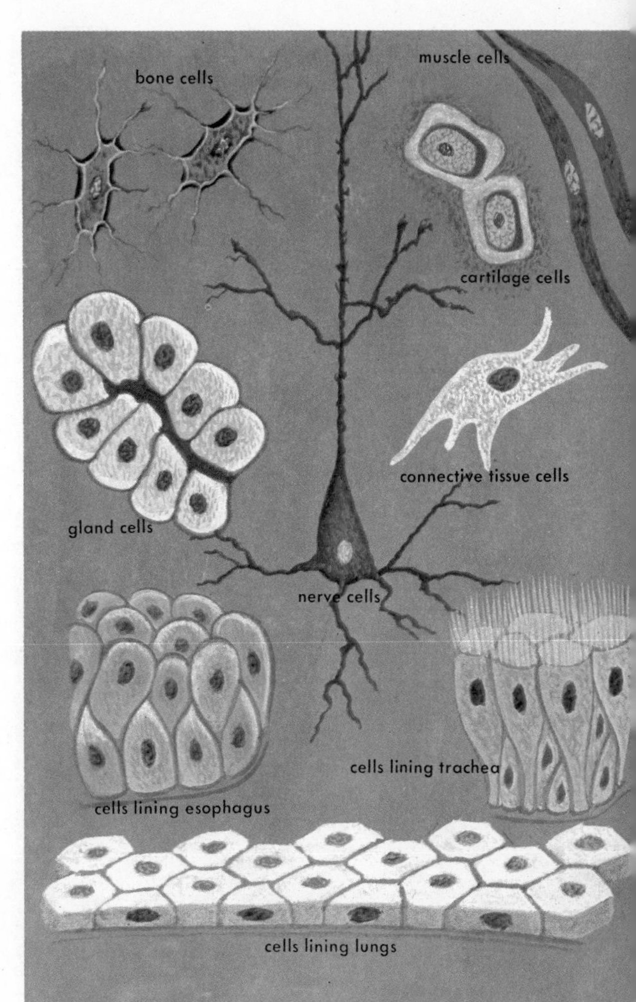

The body is made up of billions of single cells, of which there are different kinds.

Just as cells form tissues, tissues form organs, and organs form systems. All of the systems together form the human body.

The Skin

The outer layer of the skin has a name that goes back to ancient Greek days: *epidermis,* which means "outer skin." The epidermis is a form of protective armor. Single cells are fluid and must live in fluid. But because the body must live in air, there is need for a covering to contain the body's fluids. This covering is really several layers of dead skin cells stretched out and flattened.

Every day, these layers of skin are rubbed off and replaced by the layer underneath. All during the body's lifetime, the under layer of the skin continually creates new cells. This is one of the reasons why a cut on the finger, for example, heals over very quickly. Even a scrape or bruise that covers a fairly large area heals in a short time.

Underneath the outer layer is a much deeper one which is called the dermis. It is in the dermis that most of the marvelous powers of the skin come into play. For example, if the outer skin is to stay supple and strong, it must be constantly oiled. Oil glands in the skin, connected with the hair roots, do this job.

Each hair has a root that goes down into the dermis through a special shaft. This shaft is called a hair follicle. Each follicle is connected to a gland, the sebaceous gland, which pours an oil liquid into it. The liquid runs up along the hair follicle and reaches the outer surface of the skin.

The skin not only keeps itself oiled; it also helps to keep the temperature of the body steady. This is done by means of the sweat glands. These little sacs, deep in the dermis, produce a fluid that by evaporation helps to control body

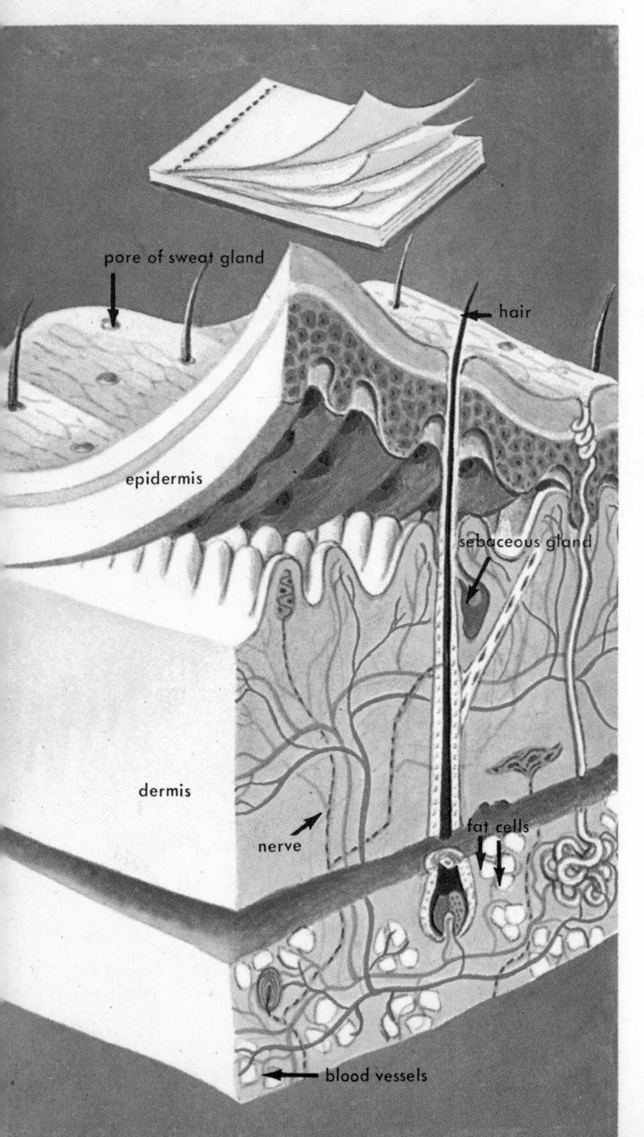

The human skin is formed of different layers, like a pad of note paper.

temperature. By means of a twisting tube, each gland's fluid reaches the outer skin through an opening called a pore. When the body is hot, from hard work or sunshine, the pores open up and sweat flows out over the skin. When the body is cold, the pores close up and no sweat reaches the skin.

There are cells of still another type in the skin, which determine the skin's color. They manufacture a substance called melanin, a dark pigment. The amount of it in the skin of a person depends mostly on the color of his parents' skin. It also depends on the amount of sunlight the person gets and on substances called hormones.

Sunlight makes these special cells more active and in this way may cause the skin to turn brown. Sometimes only small areas are affected, and when this happens a person is said to be freckled.

The skin is the frontier between the body and the outer world. Imbedded in its surface are a large number of tiny organs called sense organs, which are connected to nerve endings. These sense organs and nerve endings warn us away from things that are too hot or too cold, and enable us to have a sense of touch. They detect sensations in the world around us and transmit impulses to the brain where the sensations are identified. Because of its sense organs, the body can recognize dangerous sensations and act to avoid injury. Just as the cell's membrane protects the cell, the skin protects the body.

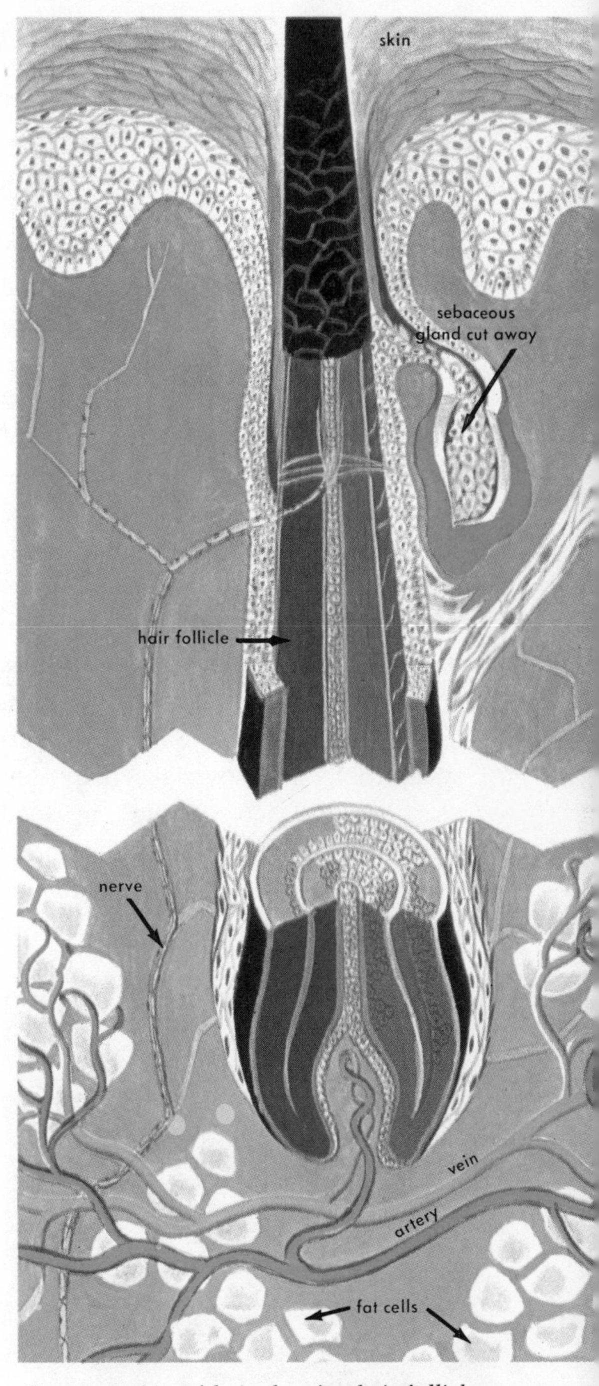

Cutaway view of hair showing hair follicle, blood vessels, nerves, and sebaceous gland.

The Systems of the Body

The human body needs many systems to allow it to function. In general, it is possible to group the organs of the body into ten major systems.

To begin with, the framework of the human body consists of 206 bones. The SKELETAL SYSTEM includes not only the bones, but the connective tissue that holds them together. Parts of the body must be able to move, so the bones are not attached rigidly but are connected by joints that allow movement.

Bones can move only when they are pulled. Tough tissue called muscles does this work. Man has over 600 muscles in the MUSCLE SYSTEM. This system not only moves the body, but also has the job of pushing food through the body and, since the heart is a muscle, making the blood circulate through the body.

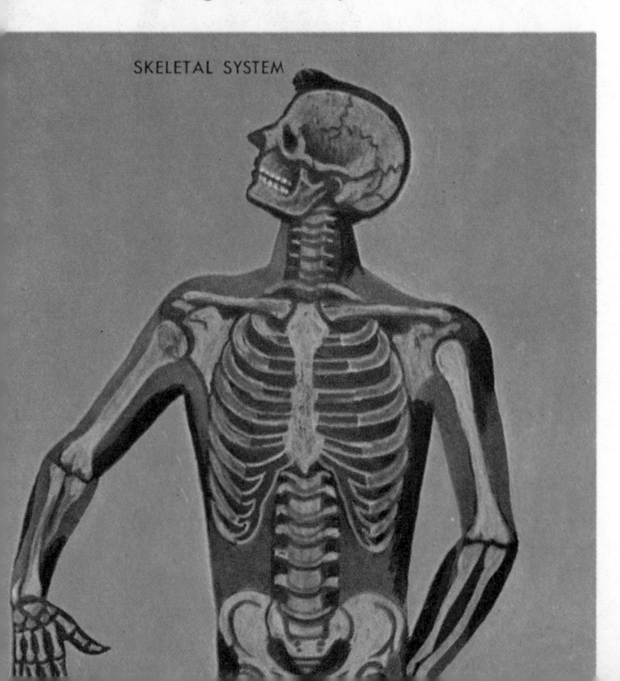

A muscle moves a bone when it is signaled to do so by the brain. The brain decides to make a particular movement because it has received a signal that calls for such a movement. It is as if the body were equipped with a combined radio-television-telephone network. We call it the NERVOUS SYSTEM. Nerves in the skin that react to heat and cold are part of this system. The eyes use part of the system when they send messages to the brain describing what is seen. The ear, the nose, and the tongue use the system to send messages describing what is heard, smelled, and tasted. It is your nervous system that tells you what you are reading at this very moment.

Movement of the body means that the body is working and therefore using energy. This energy is replaced by energy we get from food. The DIGESTIVE SYSTEM is the name of the group of organs that break up food so that it can be absorbed to supply energy for living and working.

The body must also eliminate waste products. It does this through the EXCRETORY SYSTEM. The skin eliminates salts and water. The kidneys dispose of urine. The large intestine eliminates solid wastes, and the lungs discharge water vapor and carbon dioxide.

For the body to use the energy it

gets from food, a substance called oxygen is needed. Oxygen is an invisible gas that is present in the air around us, but it is mixed with other gases which the body does not need. Oxygen must be separated from the rest of the gases. The body has a special system which includes the nose, the throat, the windpipe, the bronchial tubes, and the lungs – the RESPIRATORY SYSTEM – to deliver air into the body, where oxygen is extracted.

The energy-producing substances taken from the food by the digestive system and the oxygen separated from the air by the respiratory system have to be circulated through the body as rapidly and thoroughly as possible. Blood is the fluid that does the job. The CIRCULATORY SYSTEM, consisting of tubes of tissue called veins and arteries, directs the blood to all parts of the body. The blood moves through the arteries, passes through tubes called capillaries, then goes into the veins. It flows through the circulatory system because it is pumped by an organ of muscle called the heart and by muscles in the blood vessels.

Even though the blood vessels branch out to all parts of the body, the food that is circulated does not pass directly from the blood to the individual cells. A colorless fluid called lymph is squeezed out of the tiniest blood vessels, and it is the lymph that bathes the individual cells of tissue and supplies them with food. The LYMPHATIC SYSTEM consists of the lymph fluid, the lymph vessels, and the lymph glands.

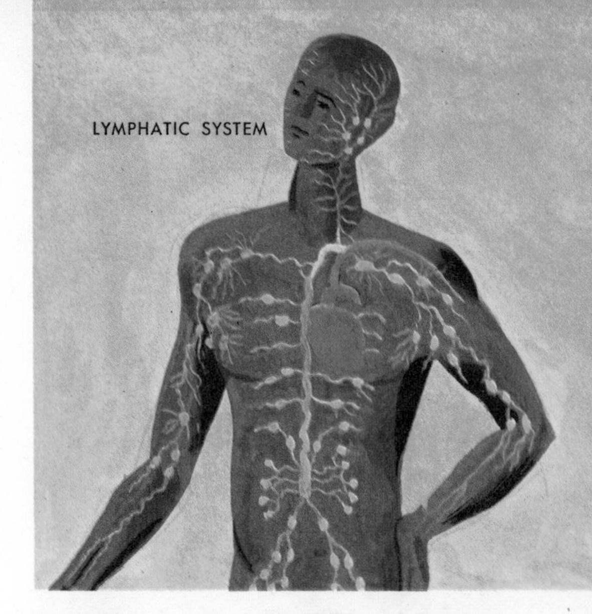

The different systems are themselves controlled by the nervous system, as well as by another system which sees to it that they all work at the proper rate. Substances known as hormones circulate through the body by means of the bloodstream. These hormones act as messengers to the different systems, regulating their activities to satisfy the body's needs from moment to moment. The ENDOCRINE SYSTEM produces these hormones from the endocrine glands.

As the body goes about its work of living, cells and tissues wear out and are continually replaced by new cells. This repair work is possible because many cells can reproduce themselves. However, the body is also able to reproduce a completely new living creature almost exactly like itself. The REPRODUCTIVE SYSTEM provides for this.

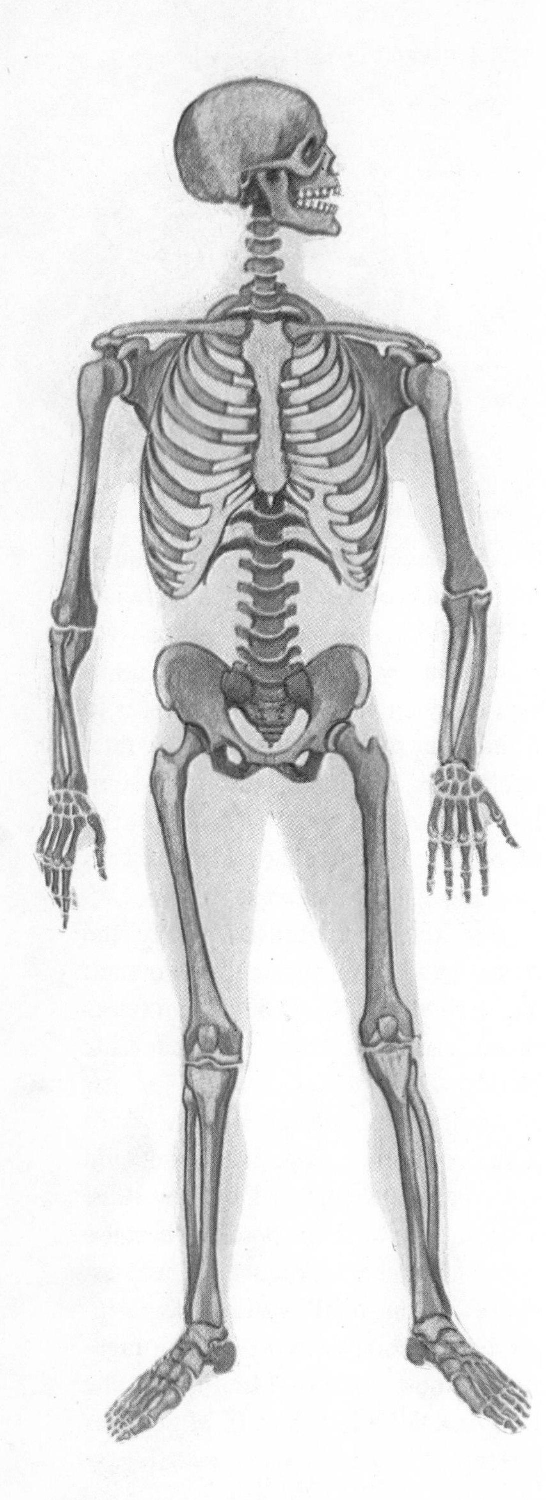

The Bones

No part of the body has just one job. The skin heals itself, oils itself, and heats and cools the body. In the same way, the bones have a great number of things to do at the same time. They are not at all as simple as they look.

The 206 bones of the human body may be roughly divided into two kinds. Touch your head, your shoulder blades, and your hips. These are flat bones. The second kind includes those we have in our arms and legs; long bones. All living bone supports and gives shape to a particular part of the body. Bones can also act as rich storehouses for some of the most important chemicals the body needs; and the flat bones are busy factories where many of the cells of the bloodstream are made.

It took man thousands of years to learn some of the concepts of building that had been used all along in his own body. Although we think of the dome as one of man's great building achievements, the bones of the head—the cranium—have long formed a perfect natural dome.

Tall buildings, airplanes, and ocean liners are supported by a framework of girders. It was very long ago that men found out that even hollow girders can be very strong; but the human body was made according to this plan from the very beginning.

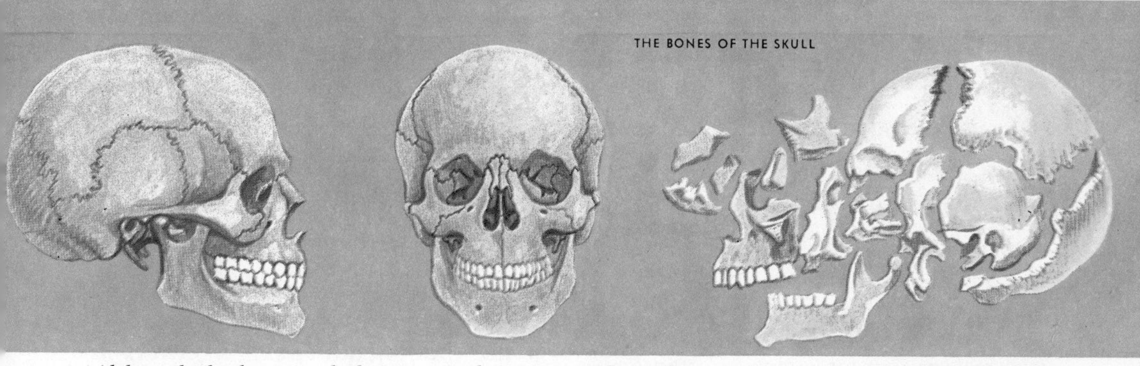

Although the human skull seems to be one simple surface, it is actually made up of a large number of smooth bones. These bones are joined together to make a perfect natural dome.

Most bones are hollow. Inside them is a soft tissue called marrow, which in the flat bones manufactures both the red and white cells of the blood. The marrow lies inside the hard, white, spongy case, the cortex, which most people think of as the bone. But even though this case looks and feels solid, it has many tiny openings for blood vessels to pass in and out bringing nourishment. Larger blood vessels also pass through the bone case, going to and from the marrow.

Two different substances, calcium and phosphorus, make up most of the cortex. Calcium makes the bone white and hard. Phosphorus is used in the nucleus of all cells. Whole milk is a good source of calcium and phosphorus. This is why growing persons need about a quart of milk a day.

In order for it to stay alive, the body is in constant need of calcium and phosphorus; and the bones give them off as needed. If, for one reason or another, the balance of calcium and phosphorus in the body is disturbed, the bones become too brittle or too hard.

Children all over the world used to suffer from a bone disease called rickets. But the discovery of vitamins showed how this disease could be cured. Doctors found that when a certain chemical called vitamin D is present, children do not develop rickets. The body makes vitamin D when the sun's rays shine on bare skin. For extra safety against rickets, vitamin D is now often added to milk or provided in special oils.

The main support of the body—the backbone—is flexible, yet powerfully strong. Run your finger up and down your spine. The little ridges tell you that the spinal column is made up of separate blocks. What you feel when you do this are little spiny projections attached to the main part of each block. The blocks are called vertebrae. Each one is fitted to the one beneath; but it is also separated from it by pads which soften the shock of movement. In the neck alone there are seven vertebrae. Twelve more vertebrae support the twelve ribs, and five very strong ones support the small of the back. In all, there are thirty-three.

In adults, the twenty-four upper vertebrae are often referred to as the "true" or "movable" vertebrae. The nine lower ones are called the "false" or "fixed" vertebrae. This is because the upper ones stay separate and flexible, while the lower ones usually unite to form two bones: the five in the small of the back forming the sacrum, the four beneath the sacrum forming the coccyx.

The backbone is made up of separate blocks called vertebrae. They fit together to give a flexible but strong support to the body.

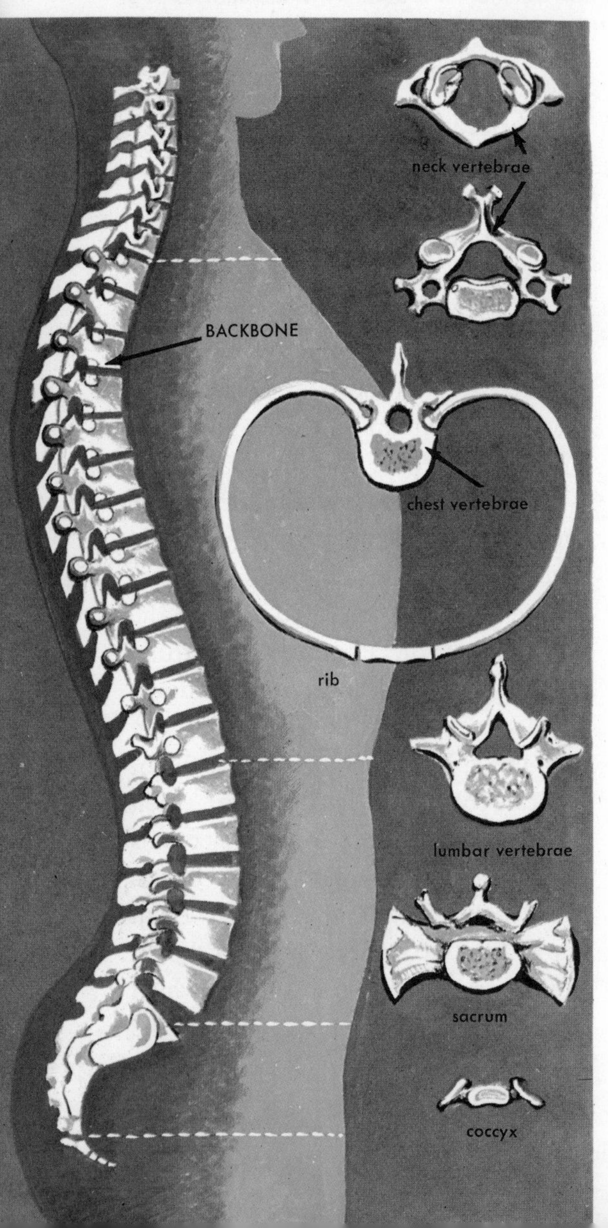

The most sensitive part of any bone is the thin membrane that covers it. This sheet of tissue contains many fine blood vessels and nerves. Bones will not heal if this covering is badly damaged.

One of the miracles of nature is the way broken bones seem to know just how to heal themselves. When a bone is broken and the two edges are brought together, the affected area is surrounded by clotted blood and the watery substance called lymph. Each edge begins to make new cells and to push them out toward the other end of the break. No one yet knows how the bone is able to throw out these strands in the right direction or why the bone continues to do this until the break is entirely healed, at which time the process stops.

In time, enough calcium is deposited around the broken ends to form a thick swelling of bone, healing the break entirely. This swelling is known as a callus. After it has healed, the bone becomes even stronger than it was before.

The thousands of movements that the body can make are possible only because of the way the ends of bones are connected with their neighbors. These connections are called joints.

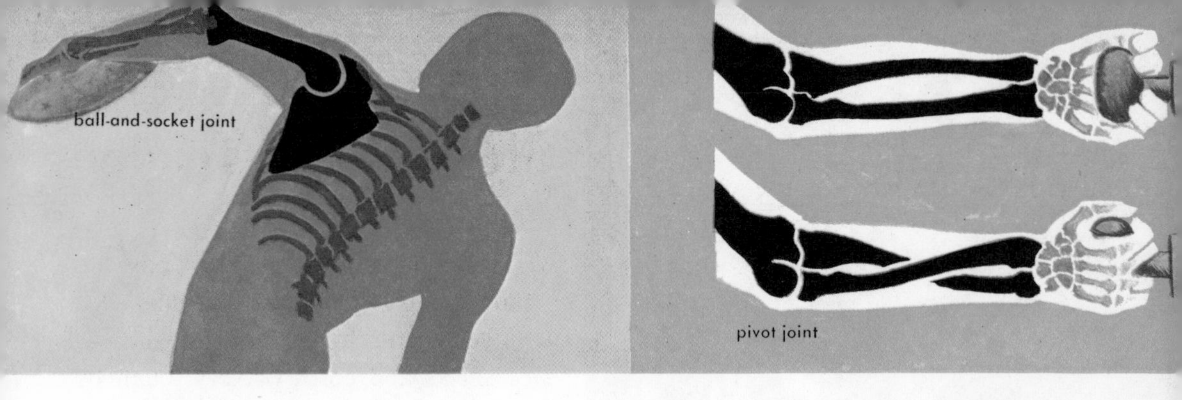

There are three principal kinds of joints. In the first, there can be no movement at all. The skull, for instance, is made up of flat bones that are closely fitted together.

In the second type of joint, only a slight movement is allowed. The spine is called a limited-movement joint because it allows a certain amount of flexibility, but not much.

The third kind of joint includes the highly movable joints of the arms, legs, hands, and fingers. There are different types of these movable joints. Twist your forearm and see how the joint at the elbow works. This joint works like a pivot.

The most movable of all joints are in the hips and shoulders. This kind of joint is called a ball-and-socket joint.

The ends of the bones are so shaped that they slide easily over each other. The ends of bones are faced with cartilage, which is smoother than bone. The cartilage lies underneath the membrane of the joint. There are also membranes that give out a special fluid which fills the joint space. When something goes wrong with these membranes, and the joint is dry, movement can be very painful.

Joints would not stay in position or last long if their parts were not lashed together to hold them steady. The ligaments take care of this. Ligaments are tough, fibrous sheets of tissue that surround the joints. Sometimes they form strips that connect the various parts of the joint. They steady the joint and allow it to move only the way that it is supposed to.

There is one type of movement that does not occur anywhere in the human body. This movement is pure rotation. There is no part of the body that can whirl around like a wheel.

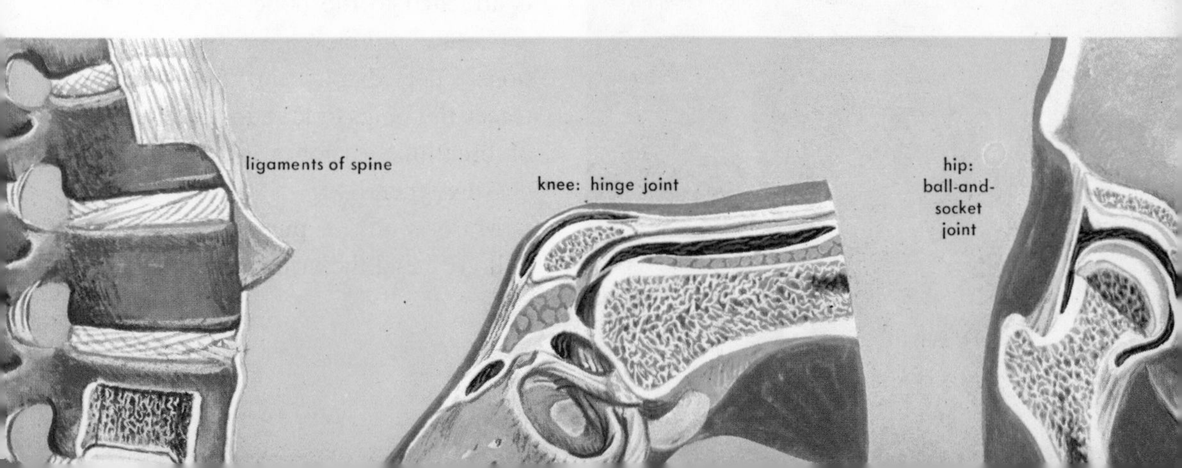

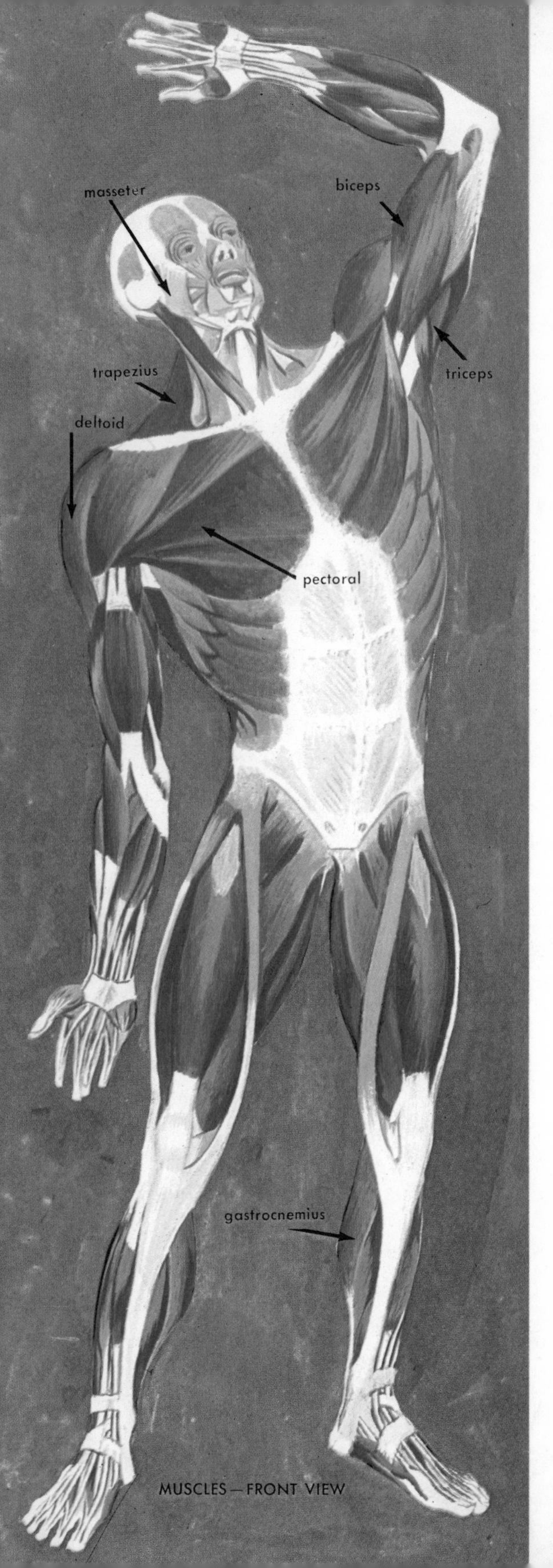

MUSCLES—FRONT VIEW

Muscles and Tendons

It is in the joints of the body that movements of the bones take place. The movement itself is caused by the pull of sheets and cords of very tough tissue called muscle. Muscle tissue has the special ability to shorten itself so that the bone on which it pulls has to move. When muscle tissue shortens, it also bunches up.

Muscle tissue covers the body in sheets and bands that lie between the skin and the skeleton. The bones are the framework of the body, but the muscles fill out the body shape. Most muscles extend from one bone to another. Suppose two bones are connected by muscle and one of the bones is held still. When the muscle between them shortens, the other bone has to move.

The point where the muscle is fastened to the unmoving bone is called the origin of the muscle. The point where the muscle is fastened to the bone that is to be moved is called the insertion.

Sometimes the muscle is not attached directly to the bone, but to a tough, non-stretchable cord, or tendon, which is attached to the bone.

A few muscles have special functions. The diaphragm, for example, forces the lungs to take in air. This part of breathing is not primarily a bone-moving operation.

Muscles do not push; they can only pull. To bend the arm at the elbow, the

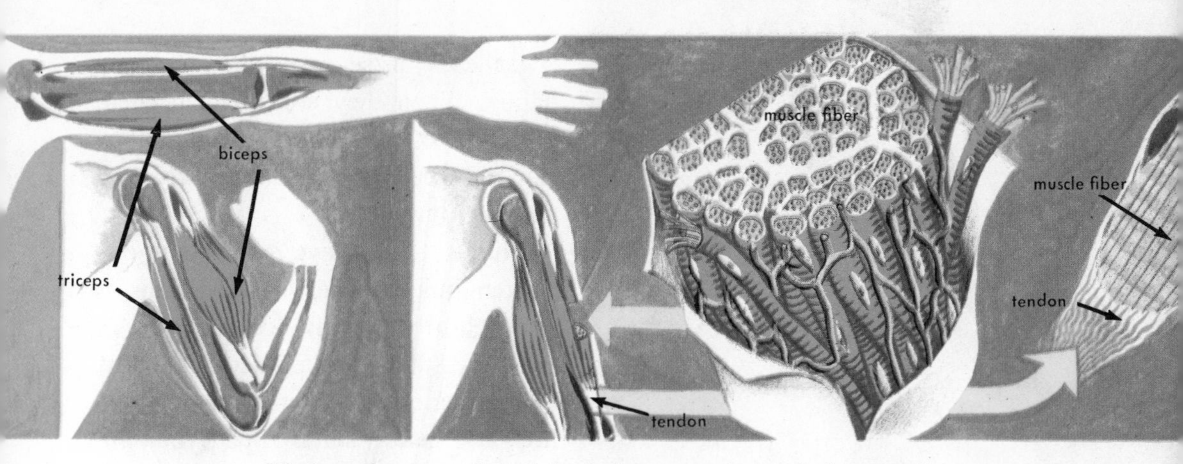

All the striped muscles of the body are made up of clusters of muscle tissue. The fibers are enclosed in individual sheaths and each muscle is itself covered by a protective membrane.

muscle at the front of the upper arm has to shorten and bunch up. To unbend the arm, other muscles in the back of the arm have to shorten.

These two sets of muscles—the front and the back—are said to act in opposition to each other. When one set is working, the other set is usually relaxed. But there are times when both of them work. Bend your arm only halfway and then use your other hand to try to force it either up or down. To keep the arm bent, you must use both sets of muscles.

Sometimes muscles are called upon to do more than simply pull in one direction. They may have to perform a turning motion. To be able to do this, the muscle must be attached to the bone at an angle. By pulling, it can cause the bone to pivot.

Some muscles are attached to bones in several places. For example, the muscle at the front of the upper arm, the biceps, has two points of attachment to the shoulder. "Bi," which means two, refers to these two points. The rear muscle which extends from the upper arm to the forearm has three points of attachment at the shoulder. This muscle is called the triceps, since "tri" means three.

Most movements of the body require the action of more than one muscle. Even to bend the arm, the biceps has to work with two other muscles.

The muscles that we can control are called voluntary muscles. They are made up of particular types of cells which are long and looked striped. The cells form long fibers of tissue, and the fibers are enclosed in a sheath. The muscles are covered with broad membranes.

Not all the muscles of the body are under voluntary control. There are also smooth muscles, so-called because they are not striped like the muscles that

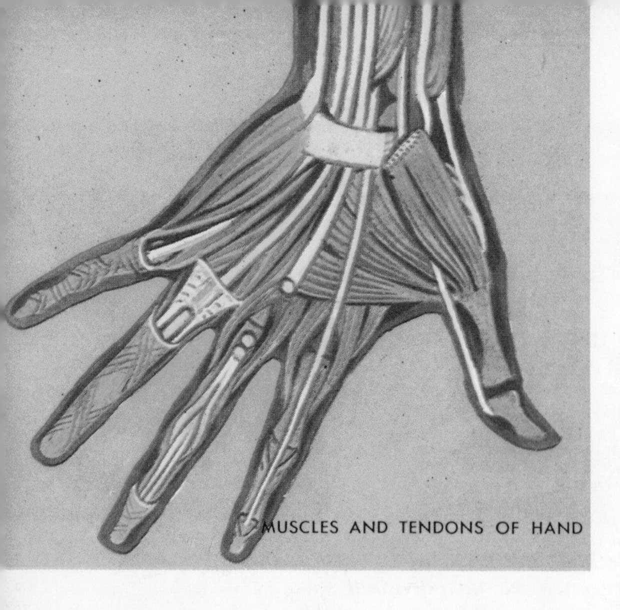

MUSCLES AND TENDONS OF HAND

we are able to control. Smooth muscle is found in the body organs and blood vessels. It narrows and widens the arteries, and pushes food through the stomach and intestines. In general, it does all the automatic moving jobs in the body. The exception is the muscle of the heart, which works automatically but looks more like the striped muscles. Smooth muscles function even when we are asleep or unconscious.

The size of the muscles in a person's body depends to a large extent on how much these muscles are used. Baseball players and ballet dancers have bulging calf muscles. Boxers have bunchy arm muscles, and their calf muscles, too, are well developed.

No one gives all his muscles equal use. For example, if you were to spend the entire day reading, you would have used your eye muscles to the point of exhaustion, but the muscles of your arms and legs would have been idle. Muscles that are never used lose what is called muscle tone—they become flabby. When they are finally needed, they are so slack and weak that they can only come into play slowly and without power.

Muscles that have good tone can tighten quickly and strongly. This is one sign of a healthy body.

Of the 206 bones in the human body, approximately one-fourth—more than fifty—are in the hands. Bend your fingers a little so that you can count just the finger bones of one hand. There are fourteen of them. It is because there are so many that the fingers are so flexible.

The palm of the hand consists of a tough, fibrous sheet lying beneath the skin, attached to the muscles of the fingers and the ligaments of the wrist. It acts as a protective shield for the muscles, tendons, and nerves that run beneath it to the fingers. If it were not present, a ball could not be caught without hurting the hand. Grasping a bat tightly would probably be painful too.

Move your wrist. Notice how easily it moves and makes possible all sorts of hand motions. The wrist is made up of eight small bones. These bones are kept in position by strong ligaments. A few of the muscles that move the fingers are attached to the bones, but their function is chiefly to make the wrist flexible.

A large number of muscles and tendons are needed to make the complicated bone structure of the hand work. Some of these start from the wrist bones and ligaments, and extend a few inches to the fingers. Many, however, start far down the forearm. You can feel them move when you clench your fist. These long muscles taper into thin, ribbon-like tendons that end in the fingers. The reason why hand and finger movements can be made with such accuracy and precision is that there are twenty-eight muscles working each hand and its fingers. Compare this with the elbow, which needs only two muscles to move it back and forth!

The master of the hand is the thumb. It stands a little away from the rest of the fingers and partly faces them. The ability to hold or grasp depends on the power with which the thumb can press against the other fingers. You can see how important the thumb is by picking up a telephone book without using it.

The human hand is wonderfully made—and so is the human foot. The foot works as if it consisted of two springs. One spring extends from the toes to the heel, and the other stretches across the foot at its widest part—just behind the toes. Usually, the base of the toes is called the ball of the foot. Anyone who has ever looked at his footprint on wet sand will have noticed that there are really two balls. One is just behind the small toe. Each toe itself also acts as a spring.

The bone structure of the foot is similar to that in the hand and wrist. The wrist, or carpus, has eight bones. The part of the foot like it, the tarsus, has seven. The foot's instep resembles the hand's arched palm and, like it, has five bones. The toes, like the fingers, have fourteen.

The complicated arrangement of muscles and ligaments already described for the hand occurs also in the foot. The main difference is that the foot, with its short toes and spring-like arches, is designed for walking, running, and jumping; the hand is designed to specialize in grasping.

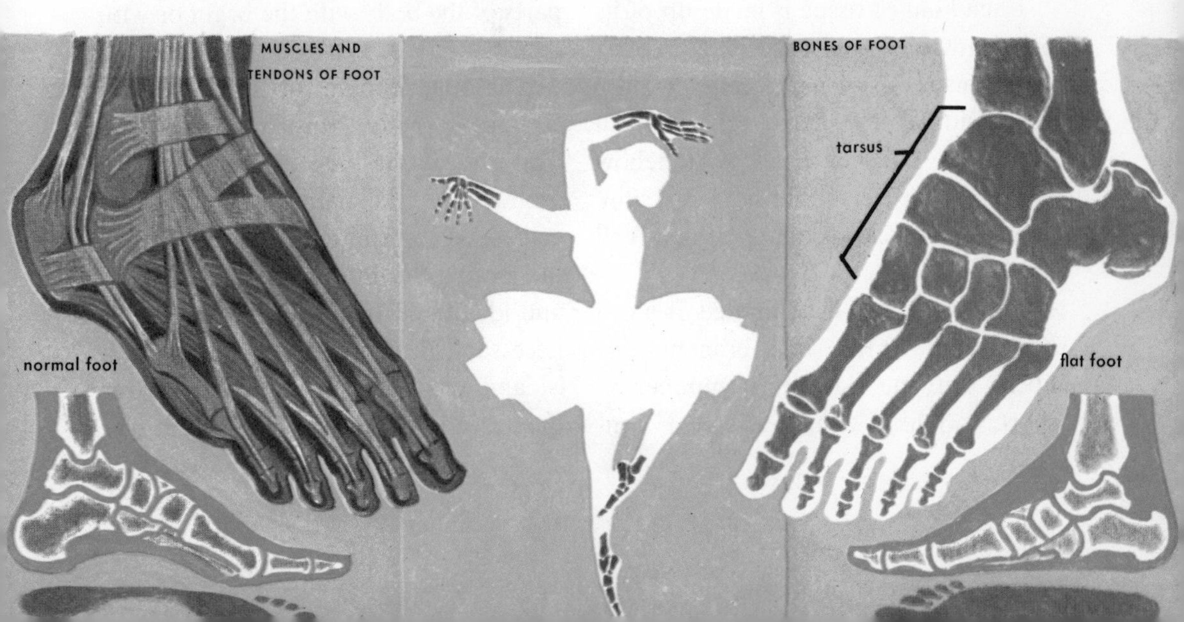

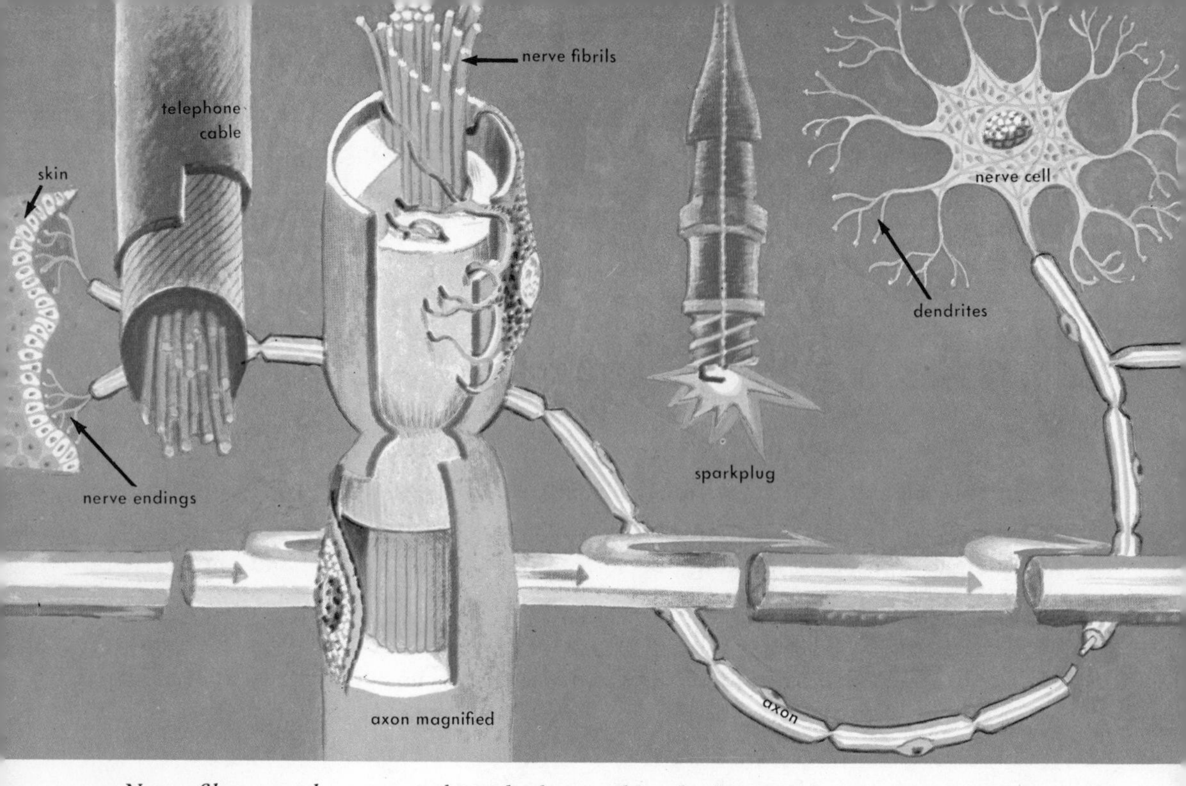

Nerve fibers may be compared to telephone cables; both transmit messages. The nerve cell is somewhat like a sparkplug, which lights up when an electrical current passes through it.

The Nervous System

Feeling anything, knowing anything, and doing anything all depend on special tissues called nerves.

Each kind of tissue is made up of its own particular kind of cells. Nerve tissue is made up of nerve cells. We are born with all the nerve cells we will ever have. If a nerve cell is somehow damaged, the nerve will not–like skin, bone, or muscle–produce a new cell to take its place.

Each nerve cell is composed of a cell body from which stem branches, or fibers. On one side are a number of short, twiglike branches called dendrites, from the Greek word for "tree." On the other side is a long branch known as the axon. The nerves connect all the parts of the body with the brain or with the spinal cord.

The outer endings of the nerves are equipped with sensitive receptors. These receptors pick up impulses and send them to the main part of the nerve cell to be transmitted to the brain. In the brain, the information is received and identified. If some sort of action is necessary, the brain determines what it is, and then sends out messages over the nerve to the muscles to carry it out.

It is clear, then, that there must be two kinds of nerves. There are nerves that carry messages of sensation to the brain. These tell the brain that the pin that sticks you hurts, or the stove you touch is hot. Because they carry messages of sensation, they are called sensory nerves. The messages from the brain are carried to muscles or glands by other nerves. These are called motor nerves because they carry messages ordering movement.

Nerves are grouped into bundles through the hollow backbone. The bundle in the backbone makes up the spinal cord.

Sometimes messages are so simple that they don't have to go all the way to the brain for a decision. For example, in the presence of something that is too hot signals telling of immediate danger go only to the spinal cord, and at once messages are sent from there to the proper muscles. Instantly the body pulls back. When the body

Some reflex actions protect us from injury.

reacts to nerve messages that do not have to go to the brain, the movement is called a reflex action.

Doctors test reflexes by tapping the knee.

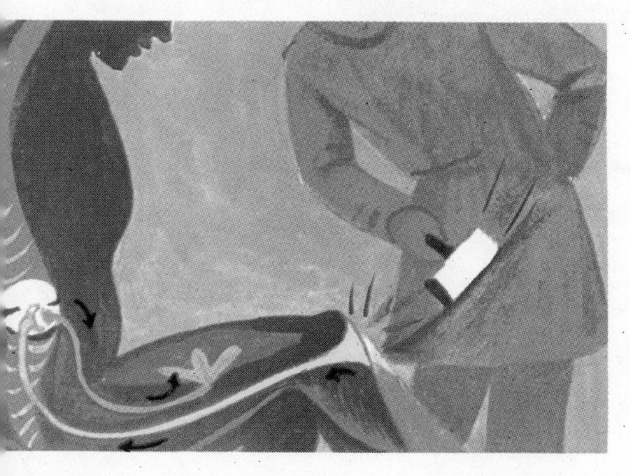

In addition to the workings of the nerves already described and to reflexes, there is another, special nervous system to take care of motions that take place automatically. In breathing, for example, muscles work to pump the air into and out of the lungs. This is done without any conscious effort by the brain. Nerves keep these muscles pumping even during sleep.

The nerves that work automatically are different from the other nerves. The muscles they control are mostly the smooth, or involuntary, muscles that were described earlier.

The people of ancient times had very little notion of the importance of the brain. They thought, for instance, that courage stemmed from the heart, and cowardice from the liver. Today we know that the brain controls all our actions. We know that the brain receives messages from all the body's organs and transmits messages to control glands and muscles.

The brain is a wonderful machine for learning. One of its greatest successes was to learn about itself. For a long time people thought that thinking was done in the heart. Now, however, we not only know that it takes place in the head, but doctors and scientists can even tell which part of the brain does a particular job.

Put one hand on your forehead and the other on the back of your head just above the neck. You are holding your brain in your hands. Then move your hands until your fingers are just behind your ears. Somewhere between the hands, the brain is connected with the spinal cord.

The surface of the brain is made of gray tissue. Underneath this layer the brain is white. Both the gray and the white parts are made of nerve tissue. Sometimes you will hear someone say of a very clever person, "He has plenty of gray matter."

The surface of the brain is slightly wrinkled in infants. As a person grows older, the wrinkles get deeper. In a full-grown man of average size, the brain weighs about three pounds. As people grow very old, the brain begins to get slightly smaller.

The part of the brain just behind the forehead is where we make plans, where we learn new things, where we remember, and where we decide between right and wrong. This part also brings together and coordinates mem-

The areas for sensation and movement in the brain (shown by human figure on brain, below) lie on opposite sides of brain's central groove. The cells that respond to stimulus in the feet are toward the top of the brain (A), while those that serve the head are lower down (B).

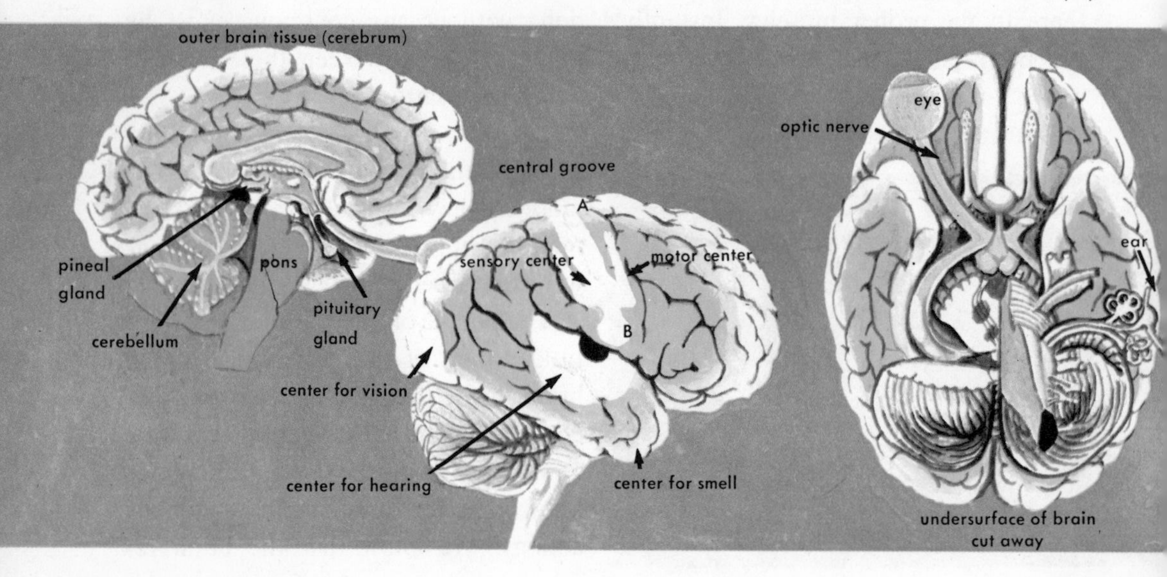

ories stored in other parts of the brain. It is the part of the brain that is much larger in man than in other animals.

About halfway back, there is a deep groove—the central groove—that separates the front part of the brain from the rear. It runs roughly on a line between the ears. Just in front of this line is the brain's motor center, the part of the brain that gives orders to the muscles to move. Doctors and students of biology know which areas control the toes, feet, legs, thighs, and so on.

Behind this deep dividing line is the part of the brain that knows where and what we feel. This is the sensory center. Just as each part of the body has a special area in the motor center to control it, so each part has a special area in the sensory center that recognizes and identifies what it feels. The brain cells in these centers may be imagined in the form of a tiny, upside-down figure on the brain (as shown in the picture, left). The cells that respond to stimulus in the lower parts of the body are toward the top of the brain, those for the upper parts of the body are lower down on the brain.

Below the sensory center, on a level with the ears, is a place in the brain that interprets sounds—the hearing center. In the back of the brain is the center for vision. The center for smell is in front of the center for hearing.

Certain parts of the brain develop more on one side than on the other. It is easy to see which side is dominant. In right-handed people, the left side of the brain is dominant. In left-handed people, it is the right side that is dominant. Some people can write or throw a ball equally well with left or right hand. They are called ambidextrous—from the Latin word meaning "double-right-handed." These people's brains are developed equally on both sides.

Underneath and behind the main part of the brain is another part, which is called the cerebellum, or "little brain." Its most important duty is to help the muscles work together. It also keeps the muscles ready to respond at once to signals to start moving. When muscles are sluggish, they don't obey nerve signals when they should. To keep our balance as we walk means that many muscles have to do their work faultlessly and in precisely the right order. Otherwise we would stumble and fall. The "little brain" keeps muscles ready to go, and coordinates them.

The twelve most important nerves in the body are called the cranial nerves, and they are in pairs—one set for each side of the body. These are the nerves that most directly report what is going on in the world about you. They all go directly to the brain.

FIRST: The nerve that carries to the brain messages about smell. The brain's center for smell, or olfactory center, recognizes several types of odors, each type having several possible variations.

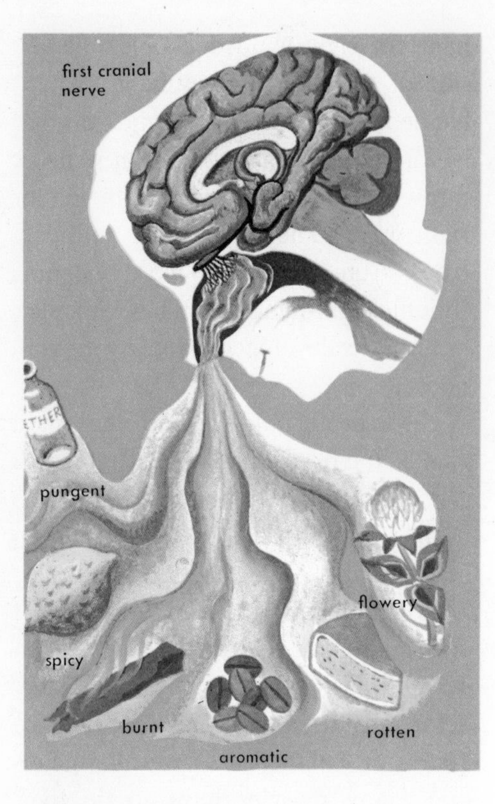

For example, one of the types of odors is called "flowery," but the olfactory center can tell the difference between violet, rose, lilac, and honeysuckle. Another type of odor is called "burnt," but the brain can tell the difference between burning tobacco, roasted coffee, wood smoke, and burning paper. A third type is that of rotting substances. A fourth may be called "spicy"; it includes such fruity odors as apple, pear, lemon, orange, pineapple, and others. A fifth type of odor includes camphor, gasoline, alcohol, turpentine, and other chemicals. A sixth is called aromatic.

SECOND: The nerve that tells the brain about what is being seen.

THIRD: The nerve that controls five of the muscles that move the eye. When you are crossing a busy street and look from side to side, it is because the brain has signaled the third cranial nerve to move the eye so that it can report any danger through the second cranial nerve.

FOURTH: The nerve that controls the upper oblique muscle of the eye.

FIFTH: A nerve with three different parts:

One part goes to the forehead and different places in the eye and the eyelid. It controls the tears in crying and when the eye needs moistening. It also tells when the nose is running, and it is through this nerve that we feel the dry tickle when the nose is dried out.

The second part of this nerve has many branches, some of which go to the side of the nose, the lower eyelid, the upper lip, and the upper gums and teeth. It also goes to the palate and throat. If you run your tongue over your teeth to moisten them the wet feeling is carried to the brain by this part of the fifth nerve.

The third part of this nerve does the same thing as the second, but for the lower jaw, the tongue, the skin of the temple, the ear, and the lower part of the face. This nerve not only carries messages to the brain, but also transmits orders from the brain to signal the jaw muscle to chew.

At mealtime, the fifth nerve is particularly busy. It carries orders to chew,

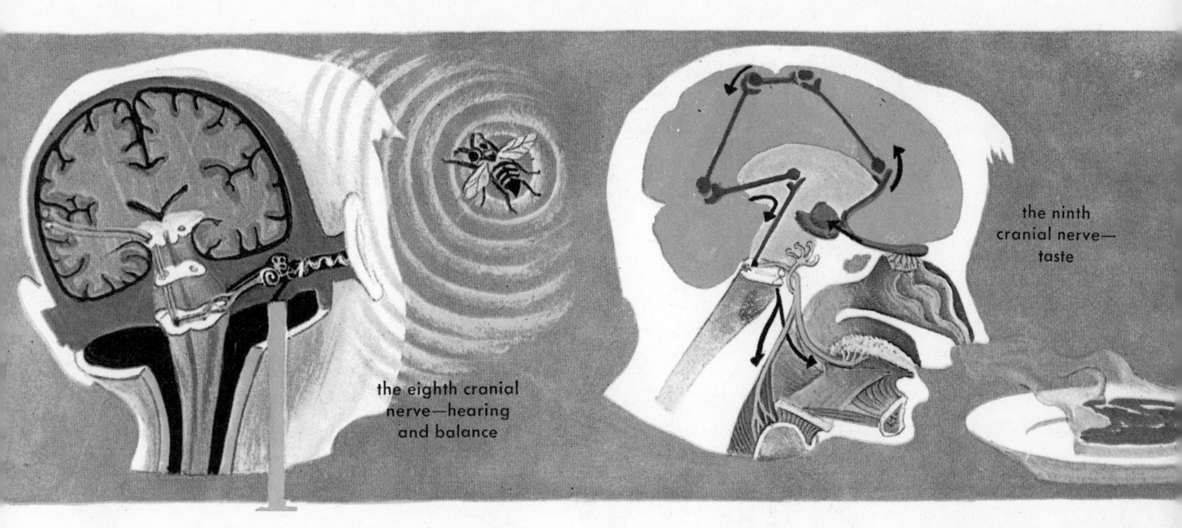

and also brings back the description of what it feels like to chew. In addition, if a cavity has formed in one of the teeth, it is the fifth nerve that aches with the news.

SIXTH: The nerve that controls the lateral muscle of the eye.

SEVENTH: The nerve that controls the muscles of your face—to make you smile, for instance. It also brings taste sensations from the front part of the tongue to the brain.

EIGHTH: The nerve that carries to the brain the news we get by hearing. It has another part which tells the brain whether or not the body is balanced or falling, and in what direction it's going. It finds these things out from a tiny balance organ in the skull near the ear. When you stumble and then manage to regain your balance, it is because the eighth nerve has told your brain about the trouble, and your brain has signaled to your arms and legs to take care of the matter.

NINTH: A nerve that has several jobs. One part of it goes to the tongue and, together with a branch of the seventh nerve, tells the brain what you taste. When you eat a piece of steak, for instance, it is this ninth nerve that tells the brain what steak tastes like. The fifth tells the brain how the steak feels to the teeth and jaws. The ninth has still another job: with the twelfth nerve, it controls the muscles of speech and allows you, when you hold out your plate, to ask for more.

TENTH: The only cranial nerve that passes into the chest and abdomen. It regulates heartbeat, breathing, and digestion without our having to stop to think about it to keep the body alive.

ELEVENTH: The nerve that carries signals to the muscles of the neck and back that turn the head and shoulders.

TWELFTH. The nerve that carries messages of movement to the tongue. You use it to talk, and to put out your tongue for the doctor.

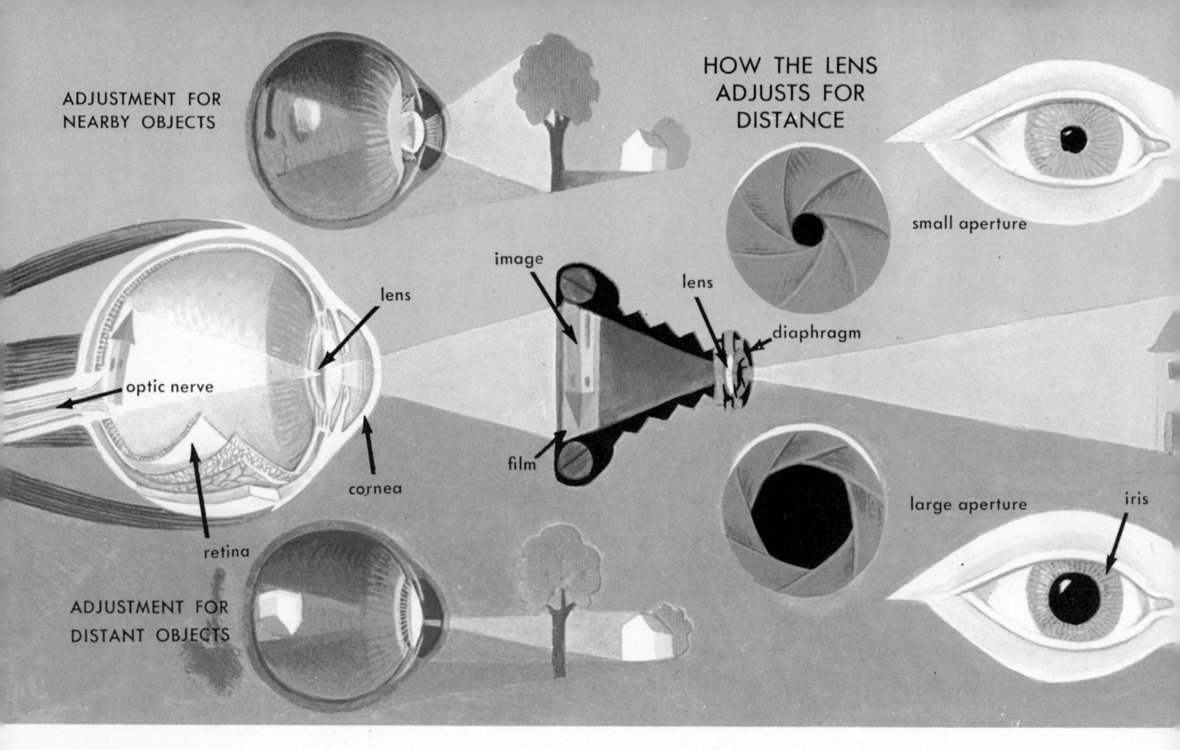

Seeing the World

In the eye, the lens, just behind the cornea, allows light to shine on a layer of tissue at the back of the eyeball. This tissue, the retina, is covered by a network of blood vessels and is changed by light shining on it. The retina is a layer of very fine nerve cells of two kinds. Some of these cells are shaped like tiny rods and recognize dimly outlined objects. Others, shaped like cones, distinguish colors and give sharp focus to vision.

Once the light reaches the rods and cones, the eye sends the message of what it sees to the optic nerve. It is along this cable that sight messages are sent to the brain.

The lens is protected by a covering, the cornea. Between the lens and the retina is a clear, thick liquid filling the ball of the eye. This liquid helps the lens bend the light to form a large picture of the scene in front of the eye.

Six muscles move each eye—up and down, from side to side. Another set of muscles, attached to each lens, make the lens thick for viewing nearby objects, or thin for distant ones. Still other muscles widen or narrow the opening of the eye to let in the proper amount of light.

The eye is set well within the head and is protected by the bones of the skull.

The Ear

Sound is vibration of the air. The ear is able to hear because it changes air vibrations into nerve messages which it sends to the brain.

The outer ear is really a funnel which collects the sound vibrations from the outside world. The ear funnel ends in a cave hollowed out of the skull inside the head, This cave, called the middle ear, is closed by a thin, tight sheet of tissue called the eardrum. Vibrating sound makes it flutter.

On the inner side of the eardrum is a set of three bones in a row. Because of their shapes, these small bones are called "hammer," "anvil," and "stirrup." The fluttering of the eardrum makes the hammer beat on the anvil, and the anvil vibrates against the stirrup, which is anchored by fibrous tissue to the opening of the inner ear still deeper in the skull.

In the inner ear are two unrelated parts: the cochlea, which houses the true organ of hearing, and the semicircular canals, which help us to maintain balance. Cochlea means "snail's shell" in Latin, which is how it looks.

The inner ear is entirely filled with fluid. The vibrating waves of sound in the air cause the stirrup bone to vibrate against the membrane that separates the middle and inner ear. This causes waves to be set up in the fluid of the inner ear. The waves pass over the cells and the sensitive, hairlike nerve endings in the cochlea, where they are converted into nerve impulses that are taken to the brain by the eighth cranial nerve.

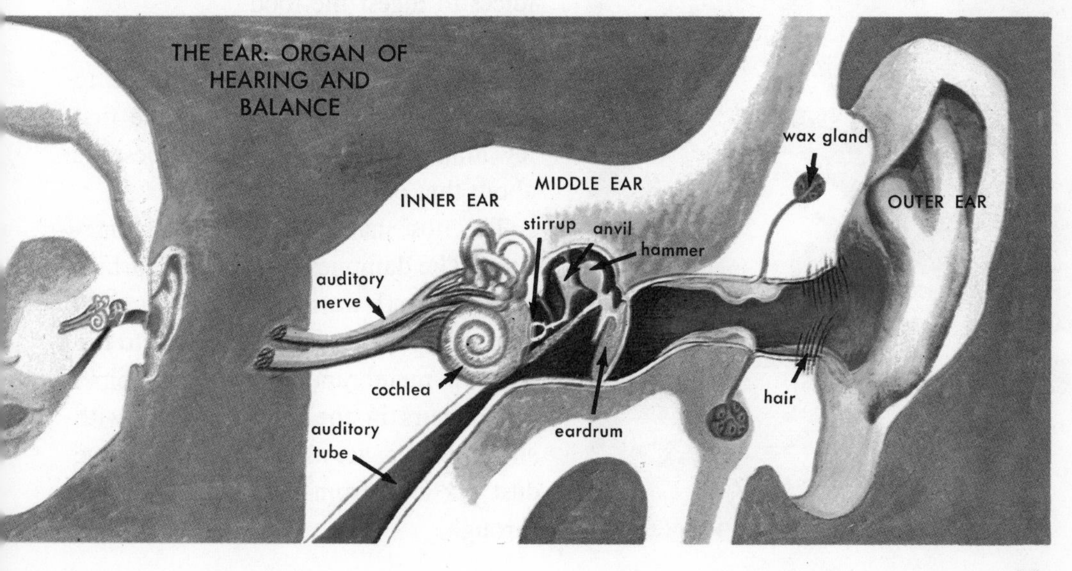

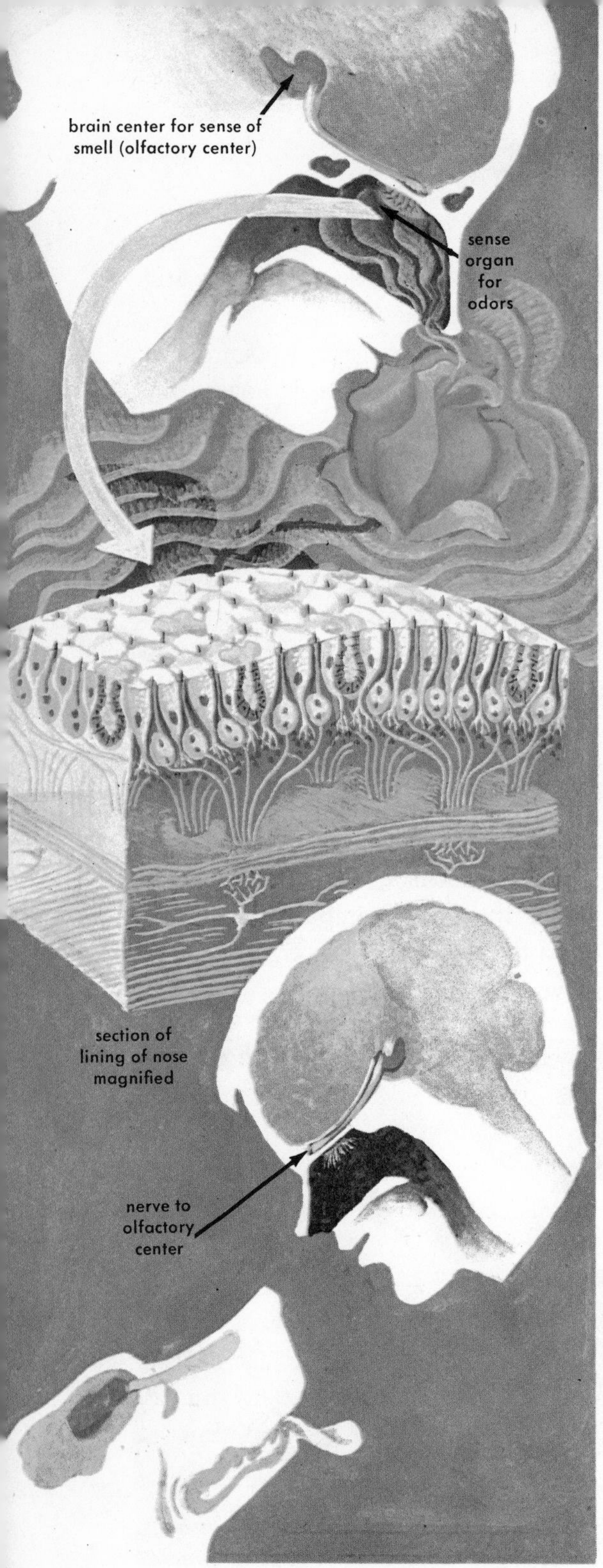

brain center for sense of smell (olfactory center)

sense organ for odors

section of lining of nose magnified

nerve to olfactory center

The Sense of Smell

The fleshy part of the nose is only an outside covering. The section of the nose that detects odors is well inside the face.

You cannot smell anything if the lining of your nose is dry. Cells are so made that they really belong to a fluid world, and this is true of the nerve cells that pick up odors. Usually the inside of the nose is lined with a thin layer of fluid called mucus. Any substance that gives off odors releases them in the form of tiny particles of vapor or gas. When these particles reach the nose, they are moistened by the mucus. Then they can be smelled.

The nerves of smell also carry the message of pleasant food to the brain. The brain then sends the signal to the stomach to be ready to give out special juices to digest the food.

The sense of smell has one peculiarity. The nerve cell becomes accustomed to an odor so quickly that after the first few minutes it stops sending the message about that odor to the brain.

The nose has other important functions. The dampness in its inner surface moistens and warms the air going to the lungs, making it less irritating to the delicate membranes of the windpipe. Small hairs in the nose, covered with sticky mucus, act as strainers to remove dust particles from the air as it passes through.

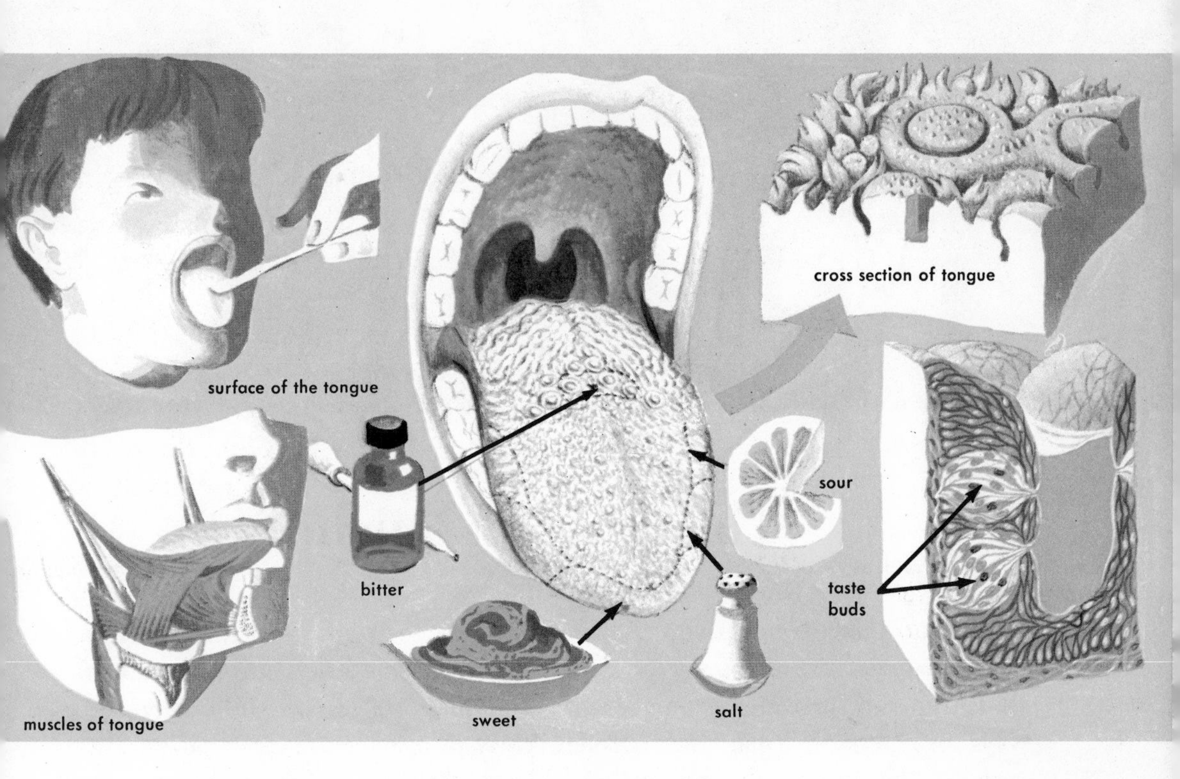

The Taste Buds

The sense of taste is located in the tongue, which does the tasting by means of special cells, called taste buds, on its surface. Human beings have about 3000 taste buds.

Taste buds all look alike, but doctors think there are four different types, one for each of the primary tastes—sweet, sour, bitter, and salt. The buds for these four primary tastes are grouped in special places. The front, or tip of the tongue, picks out all flavors, but particularly salt and sweet. Sour substances are best tasted along the sides of the tongue, and bitter things toward the back.

However, most of the flavor of food is recognized by the sense of smell. When the nose is clogged up, all food tastes flat even though the taste buds may be working perfectly normally.

The receptors for the sense of taste cannot work at all unless the substance they are working on is in a fluid state. However, the tongue is covered by a special liquid that flows into the mouth from glands in the cheeks and under the tongue. This liquid, which is mostly water, is saliva. Food particles are moistened by saliva, and then they can be tasted.

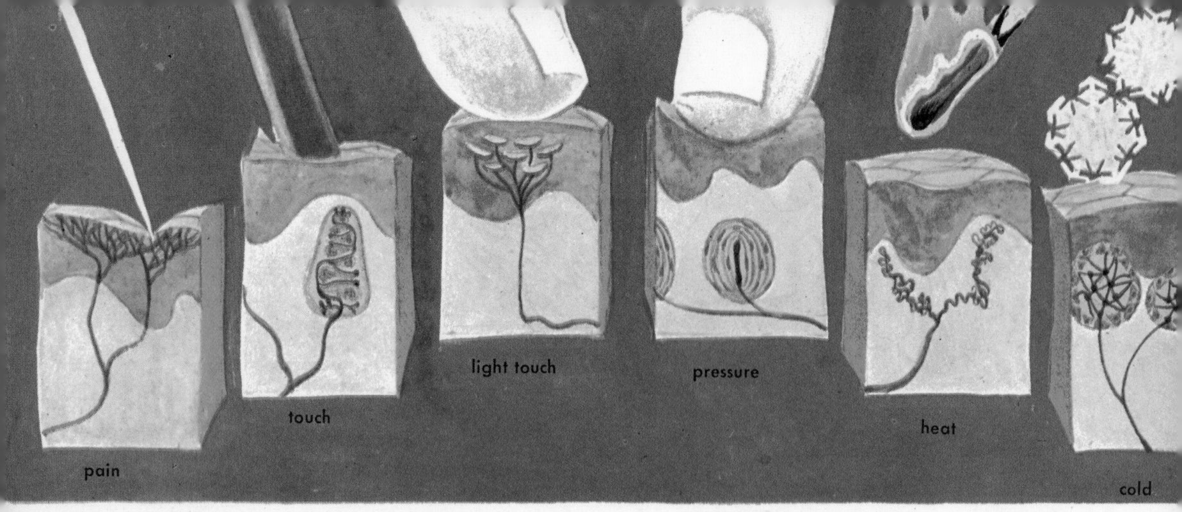

The Sense of Touch

All that stands between you and the outside world, you might say, is your skin. The skin provides a number of ways of knowing what the outside world is like, and whether at any moment it is a safe or a dangerous place. The sense of pain in your skin makes you jump away when you touch something sharp. The sense of warmth makes you back away from too much heat. When it is cold, your skin warns you to put on more clothing. This is simply another way of saying that the skin, by its ability to feel different sensations, protects the body from harm.

The skin reports these sensations through special organs imbedded in it. Each organ is specialized to detect cold, warmth, pain, or simple pressure. These tiny warning devices work somewhat like electric push buttons that send signals through the nerves to the spinal cord, and eventually to the brain. If the signal is painful, as from a pin prick or a hot stove, a reflex action may be set up. If a hand gets close to a hot stove, for example, this is reported to the nervous system. A motor nerve then stimulates the muscles to contract and withdraw the hand from the stove. In such a case the hand is withdrawn unconsciously. This is an example of a reflex action that begins in the skin.

In the skin there are twelve groups of cells to feel coldness as well as seventy-eight to feel heat. In addition, separate clusters of special sensory organs feel moving air currents, respond to stroking or tickling, or tell of movements by the skin.

So many different sensations come to us through the skin that it would be more correct to speak of perhaps a dozen senses of touch instead of only a single one.

The Digestive System

The cells that lie within the human body are made up mostly of liquid and can feed only upon liquids. To provide them with the nourishment they need, the body must convert the bulky foods we eat into a smooth, liquid paste, and separate from this paste the tiny particles on which the cells can feed. The group of organs that do this form the digestive system.

The first part of the digestive system's job is the conversion of solid food to semi-liquid form.

When food first enters the body, it is ripped, crushed, and torn by the teeth. The tongue, which is a powerful muscle, mixes and turns the food so that the teeth can break it up. At the same time, special glands in the mouth moisten the food with saliva to soften it. Saliva also starts the breaking down of certain types of food.

When the food has become soft enough, the tongue pushes it to the back of the mouth and into the throat. There, rings of muscle force it down the esophagus or upper digestive tube.

The esophagus extends almost straight down from the middle of the neck to the bottom of the chest. It is lined with the strong muscles that squeeze progressively to make sure that the food is moved in the right direction.

The food enters the stomach in a semi-liquid form, therefore the stomach needs no grinders or crushers like the teeth. Instead, it is lined with powerful muscles that mash and mix the food into a still finer paste. While the stomach is mixing the food, special cells in its walls release acids and fluids called enzymes that continue the job of breaking down food into the forms that can be fed to the cells.

The food is forced by the stomach into the intestine, when the stomach juices have done their work. Special muscles in the stomach move the partly digested food along and pass it through an opening called the pylorus, which connects with the top of the small intestine.

The small intestine is a narrow tube about twenty feet long. To allow it to fit into the space between the diaphragm and the end of the trunk, where the legs join the body, it is coiled and twisted. The tube is lined with muscles that squeeze in turn to force the food along its length.

The inside of the small intestine is lined with four or five million tiny, hairlike projections called villi. These projections provide a large surface for the absorption of the food in the intestine.

As the semi-liquid food passes through the small intestine, almost all the useful, solid particles are removed from it and passed along to the blood-

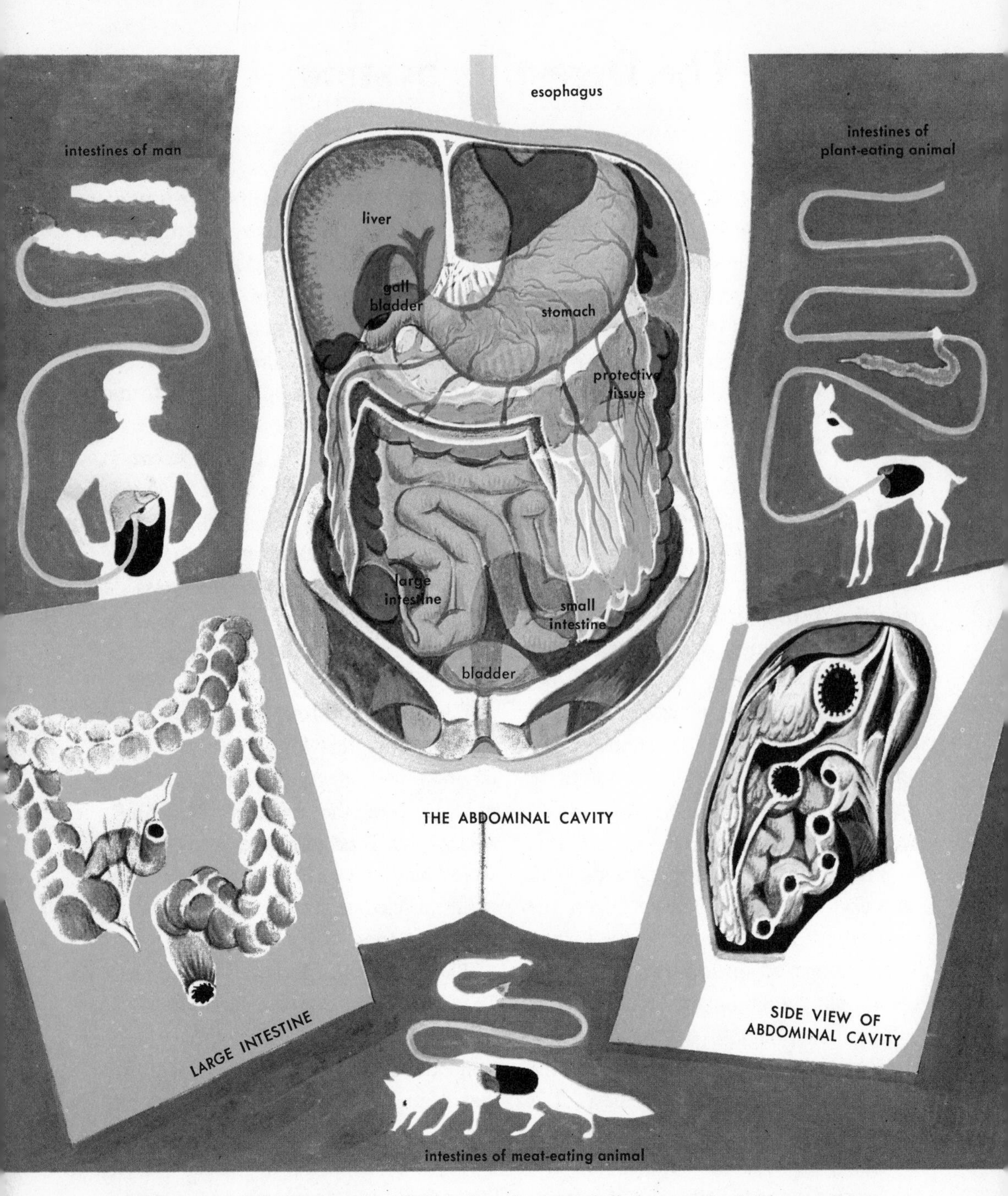

The stomach helps liquefy solid food so the body cells can use it. In the small intestine, the nutritive solid matter is removed and distributed through the body. In the large intestine, the nutritive liquids are removed and sent to the body's cells.

stream to be distributed throughout the body. The rest of the food continues through the small intestine until it reaches the lower end, where it enters the next portion of the digestive system, the large intestine.

The large intestine is wider and heavier than the small intestine, but shorter. It extends up one side of the abdominal cavity, crosses to the other side of the body, then leads down. Its job is to remove the useful liquid portion of the food. The body gets rid of the remaining solid waste matter at the end of the large intestine.

Among the organs and glands that aid digestion without actually transporting the food are the salivary glands. Also included are the liver and pancreas that give forth bile and the pancreatic juices.

Bile is produced in the liver. It is stored in the gall bladder and enters the small intestine during digestion through a small tube or duct called the bile duct. Joining this duct just before it connects with the small intestine is another, leading from the pancreas. Bile and the pancreatic juices are thus able to flow together into the intestine.

In the villi, nutritive food is taken in by lymph vessels to be distributed in the body.

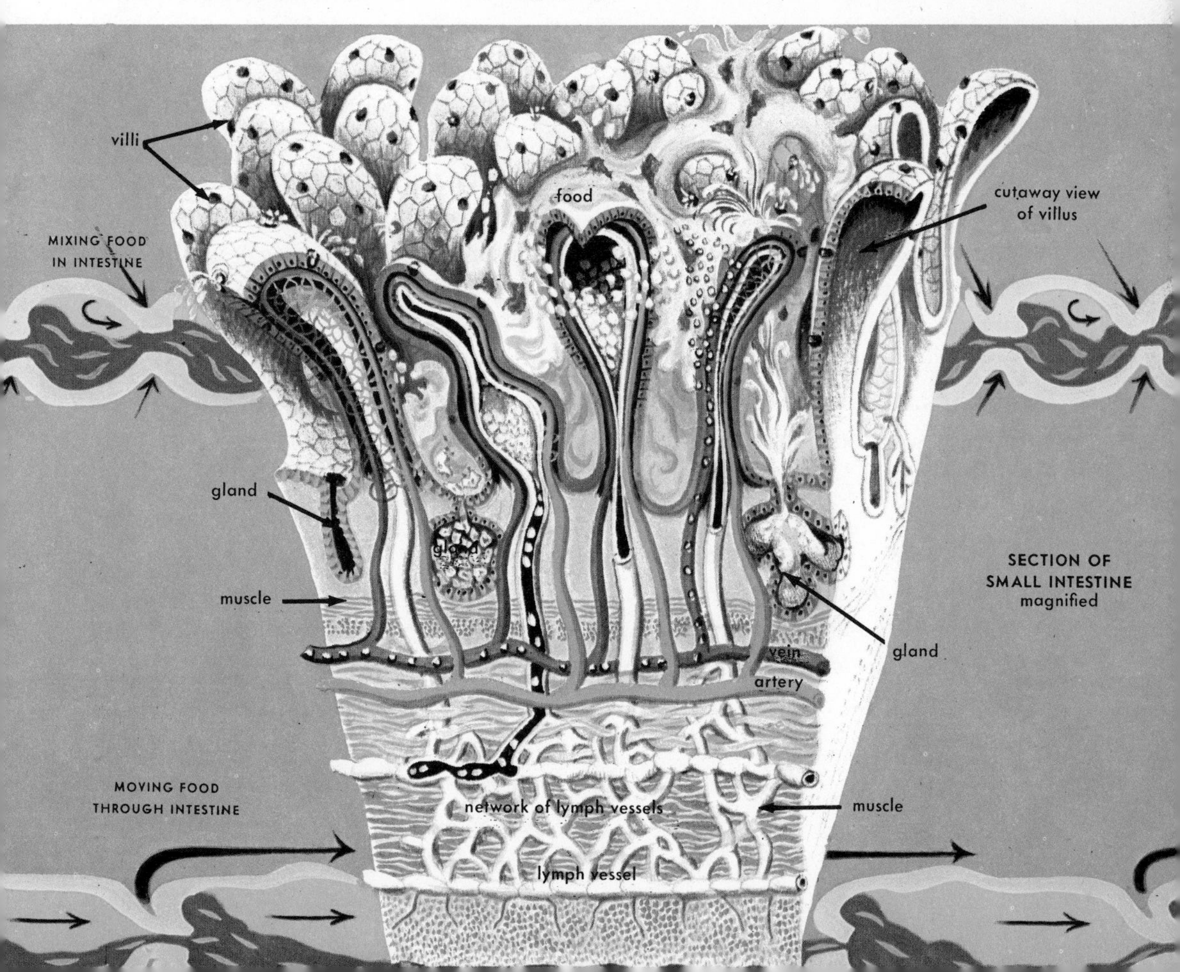

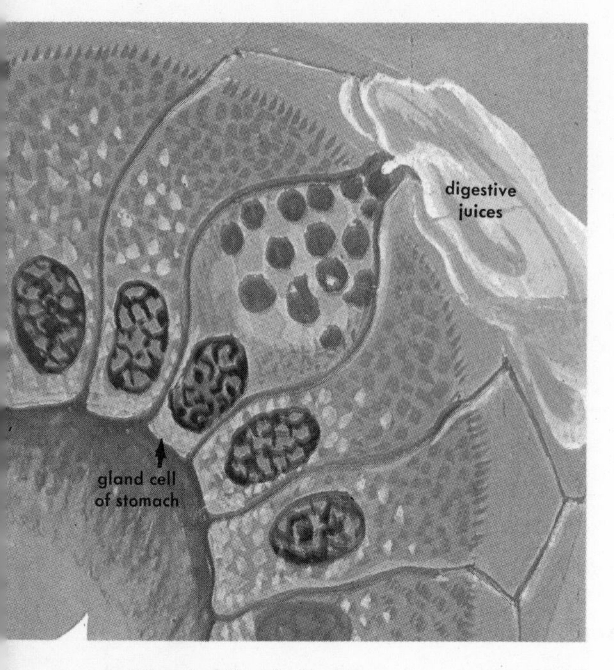

Gland cells of the stomach are stimulated to release digestive fluid.

Almost all the functions of digestion, except putting food in our mouths and chewing it, are carried on without our having to stop and think about them. These functions are controlled by the automatic nervous system in response to impulses received from the lower part of the brain and the lower spinal cord. Hormones secreted by the digestive organs themselves also help control digestion.

The digestive juices and enzymes are manufactured in the body's glands and organs, and are released when they are needed. The first digestive juice is released in the mouth. It is saliva, which contains an enzyme called amylase. The body is unable to make use of starch, but it can use certain sugars, even though both of these are carbohydrates. Amylase starts breaking down starch into a sugar the body can use.

The next stage of preparation begins a few minutes later in the stomach and goes on for over an hour. Special cells in the stomach's walls pour a little acid on the food. The acid has effect upon meat, fish, cheese, and similar foods. It also helps another digestive juice—pepsin—to change proteins into amino acids.

The stomach also pours forth another substance, mucin. Mucin coats the wall of the stomach and protects it from the digestive action of acid and pepsin. Special glands in the stomach give forth these juices as needed.

The food that leaves the stomach is still only partly ready to be taken in by the cells. The final stages of digestion are carried out in the small intestine by juices from the liver and pancreas. The liver sends bile to help break up fat. The pancreas, a large, beltlike gland lying behind the stomach and the upper part of the intestine, secretes juices that split proteins, carbohydrates, and fat. Proteins are changed into amino acids. Fats are broken down into fatty acids and glycerin. Starches and sugars become glucose.

Man's senses make his body's necessary work more fun. And the enjoyment of food actually helps digestion. Digestive glands in the mouth and stomach work better when we are relaxed and happy, and when the food is pleasing.

The Teeth

The teeth, which first crush the food in the mouth, are really a kind of bone and should be considered part of the skeleton, even though they do not have the healing ability that bone has. Fortunately, teeth are covered by the hardest material in the entire human body—enamel. This covering is so hard that teeth can take great shocks without harm. Yet enamel is one of the few tissues that cannot repair damage to itself.

Every tooth has a soft center which contains nerves and blood vessels, and every tooth is rooted in the jaw. Human beings have two sets of teeth—a set that grows in early childhood, and a much tougher, larger set that grows in and pushes out the first set. The first set numbers twenty, and is called milk teeth. The second set of thirty-two—the jaw is now large enough to hold more teeth—is called the permanent set.

The upper and lower four teeth in front of each jaw have sharp cutting edges for biting food. They are called by the Latin word *incisor,* meaning "cutter."

On either side of the incisors, both upper and lower, is a sharp-pointed tooth that looks somewhat like a dog's tooth and for that reason is called a canine tooth. There are four altogether. These teeth begin to be replaced in about the sixth year by a tougher set.

In the first set are eight teeth toward the back of the mouth for grinding food. These are called molars. Later, when the second or permanent teeth come in, we have a total of twelve new molars, along with eight other teeth between the molars and canines. These additional teeth are called bicuspids.

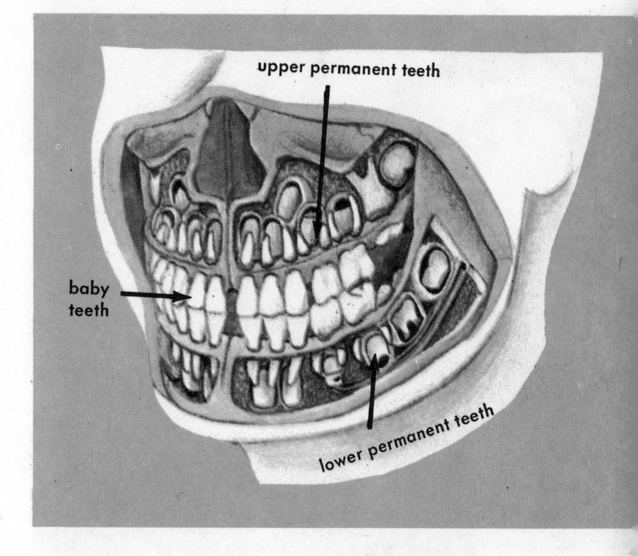

Cavities form when food particles lodge between the teeth and decay begins.

The working part of the tooth, as far as eating is concerned, is the crown. Generally, the crown is covered with an invisible layer of certain cells, called bacteria, which attack sugar. Pure sugar is turned into acid, which in turn dissolves enamel in spots. This dissolving of the enamel is the beginning of decay.

Decay usually begins in those places on the tooth where tiny particles of food are likely to be left behind after chewing. This is why it is good to brush teeth after eating.

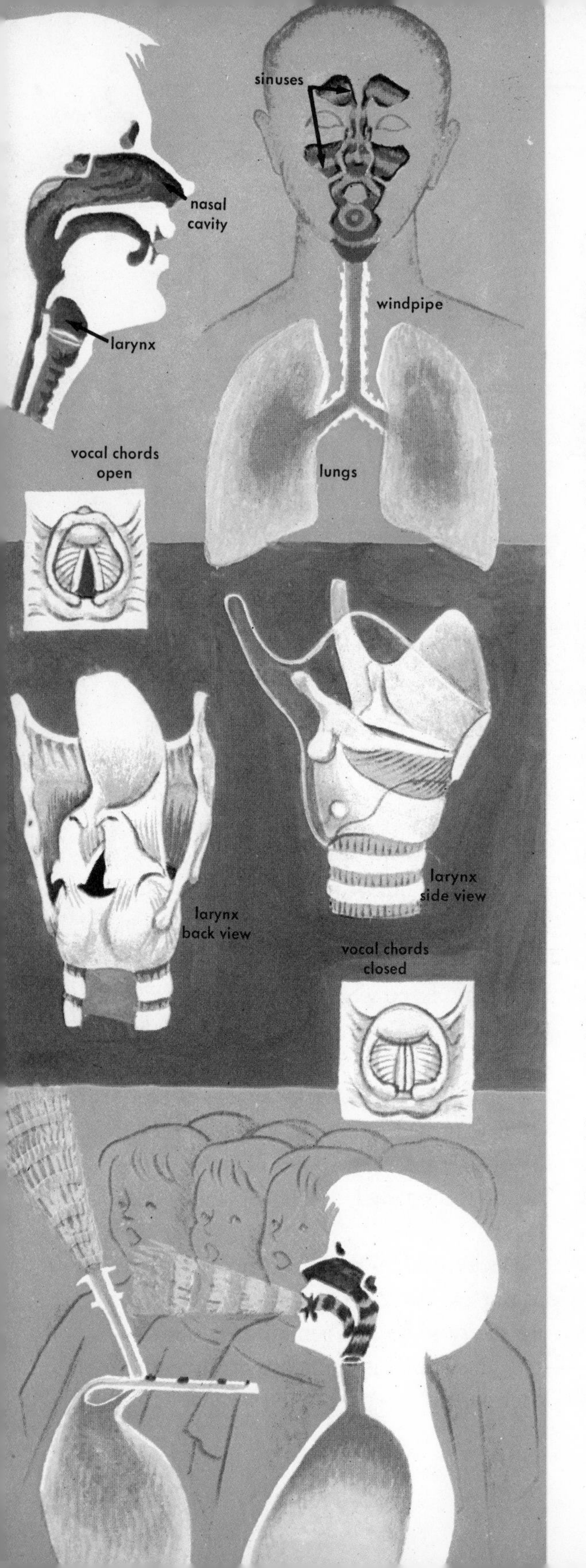

The Larynx

The larynx lies in a small cave of muscle in the front of the neck, a little below the back of the tongue. The entrance of this cave is protected from food by a little curtain of cartilage, the epiglottis. The larynx rises up against this curtain to keep out food every time you swallow.

The larynx needs only two little bands of tissue to make all the sounds in the human voice. They are stretched side by side in a V pointing toward the front of the throat. Air from the lungs passes between the edges of the two bands and makes them vibrate. This vibrating motion is what makes the sound.

When the edges of the bands are close together in a narrow V, the sound is high. When the space between them is wide, the sound is deep. The pitch of the sound also depends on how tightly or loosely the bands are held by the larynx muscles. Changes in pitch can be made quickly.

When the bands of the larynx are long and thick, all the sounds seem low and deep. This is why men have voices that are much deeper than children's.

The sounds in speech depend also on our lips, tongue, and teeth—how they are shaped and how we use them.

Air is squeezed from lungs as from a bagpipe. Vibration of air causes sound.

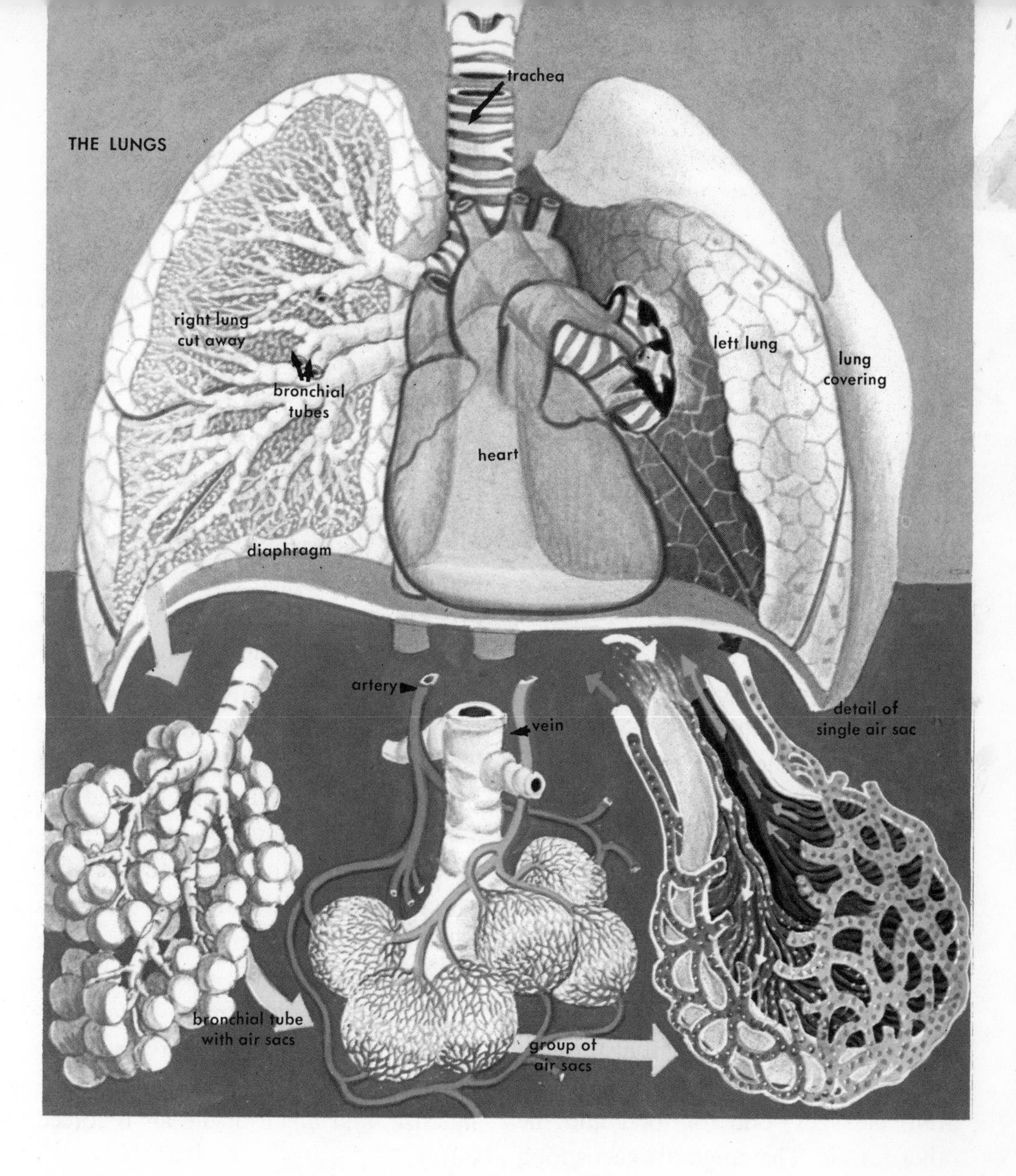

Take a Deep Breath

Life depends on breathing because the cells of the body need oxygen, which is one of the gases in the air We breathe in—inhale—to bring fresh supplies of air to the lungs, which will take the oxygen from it. We breathe out—exhale—to get rid of the other gases in the air that the body doesn't need, as well as waste gases, carbon dioxide, that the body has made while doing work.

The separation of oxygen from the air by the lungs is important and deli-

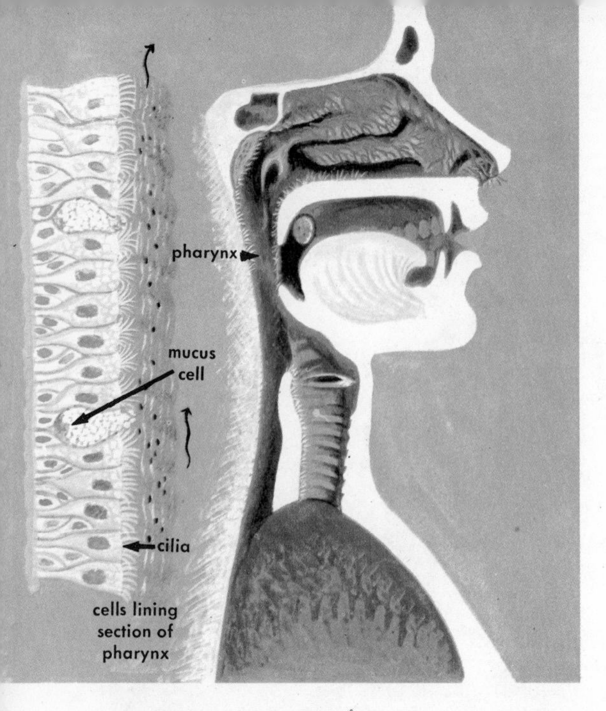

cate work. For this reason the air coming to the lungs must be as clean as possible. Air enters the body through the nostrils. Inside the nose are fine hairs and a thick fluid that catch many of the larger dust particles in the air. The nose is also lined with many fine blood vessels, which warm the air that passes through.

Air and food pass together for a short distance down the throat through a tube which then splits into two separate passages: one for food and the other for air. The epiglottis keeps food out of the passage leading to the lungs.

The windpipe is a tough muscular tube supported by rings of cartilage. It, too, is lined with hairlike projections called cilia and a fluid that traps germs and other material from the air.

The windpipe forks into two smaller pipes called bronchi or bronchial tubes. One leads to the right lung, the other to the left. These again branch into smaller and smaller tubes. The smallest branches finally lead into clusters of tiny air sacs that perform the main work of the lungs. Oxygen is taken out of the air and exchanged for carbon dioxide inside these tiny sacs.

This exchange takes places in tiny blood vessels, or capillaries, in the walls of the alveoli, or air sacs. After the carbon dioxide has passed from the blood through the capillary and alveolar walls, it is breathed out by the lungs. Oxygen breathed into the lungs goes through the alveolar and capillary walls into the bloodstream.

The lungs fit into a boxlike space. The bottom of the box is the sheet of muscle called the diaphragm, and the sides of the box are ribs and the muscles that move them. When the diaphragm moves down and the ribs spread, the lungs are stretched and air rushes in through the nose and windpipe to fill the extra space. A few seconds later the diaphragm relaxes, the lungs are squeezed back to their original size, and much of the air is forced out.

Breathing is another example of one of the body's automatic functions. However, we can breathe at any speed we want. Laughing, sucking, coughing, and blowing are all forms of controlled breathing. Most of the time, though, the body regulates breathing without our even being conscious of the rate of speed.

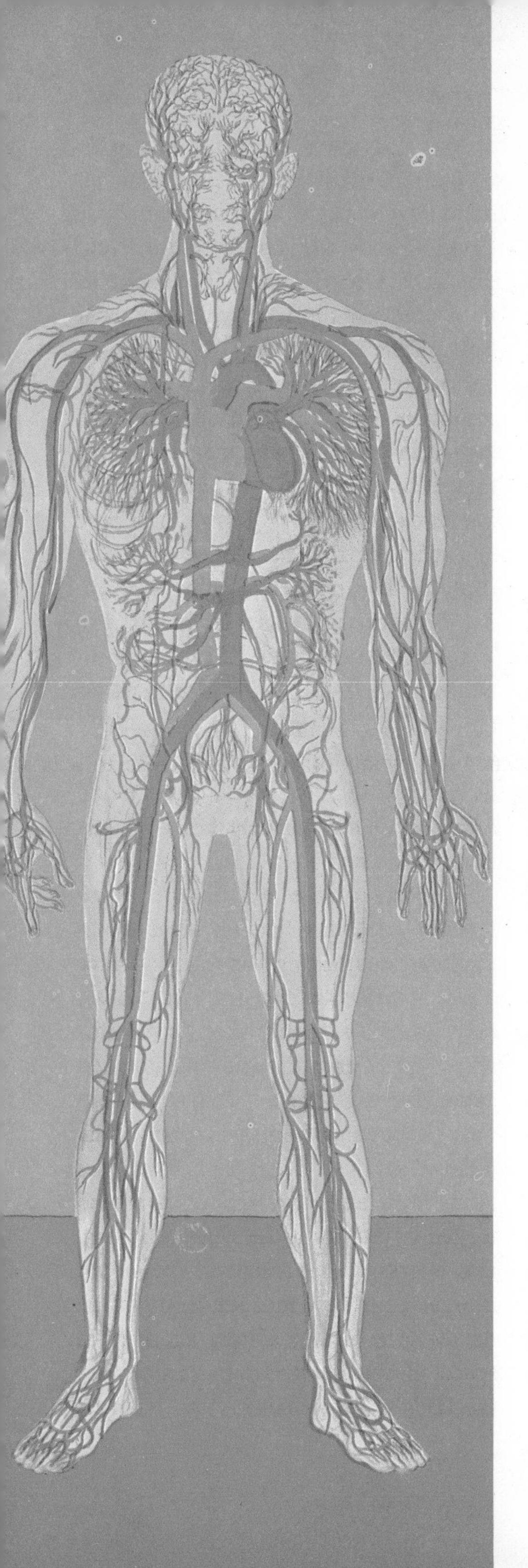

The Circulatory System

The blood is forced through the body by the pumping action of the heart, and moves through the large tubes or blood vessels called arteries. Arteries extend throughout the body. Those nearest the heart are fairly large. As they get farther away from the heart, the arteries divide and split into smaller and more numerous arteries.

As the branches of an artery become smaller and smaller, they narrow down until they are thinner than hairs. They become so thin that the blood moves through them slowly.

Because they are so narrow and hair-like, these tiny branches are called capillaries, from the Latin word for hair. In the capillaries, the slowly moving blood delivers food and oxygen to the cells. At the same time, it picks up the waste materials that the cells must get rid of.

Once it has delivered its cargo of oxygen and food and picked up its return load of waste materials, the blood continues to flow along the capillaries, which now begin to come together. Gradually there are formed larger and larger blood vessels that will return the blood to the heart. The blood vessels that take the blood back to the heart are called veins.

Look at the underside of your wrist.

Put your finger on the upper part of the wrist, close to the base of the thumb. If you find the right spot, you will feel a steady beating under the skin. This beating is the pulse, and it is caused by the flow of blood that is being pumped through one of the wrist's arteries. Each beat is caused by a beat of the heart.

Blood in the arteries is bright red. The color comes from the oxygen the arteries carry. Blood in the veins is blue because it has lost its oxygen.

The red color is due to a special protein in the blood called hemoglobin. When hemoglobin is carried to the lungs, it picks up oxygen and turns a light red. When it is pumped through the bloodstream into the body's tissues, it gives up its oxygen and becomes a darker, bluish red. Then it enters the veins and returns to the heart and lungs for a new supply of oxygen. Without hemoglobin, there would be no efficient way to transport oxygen to all the tissues of the body.

Arteries are stronger than veins. Their walls have to be thicker because the blood is pumped through them with far more force and pressure than it is pumped through the veins. Veins are more delicate, but wider.

Blood must not only be kept flowing constantly, but it must be kept flowing in the right direction. Because of this, veins have little valves spaced at intervals along their length to make sure the blood does not flow backward.

The heart is really two pumps, side by side–one on the right and one on the left. The pump on the right sends blood from the veins to the lungs. Then it pumps blood through the lungs to the pump on the left, which sends it through the body.

Each pump consists of two hollow chambers, one above the other. The two chambers are separated by valves that allow the blood to flow in only one direction.

Each time the muscles of the heart contract, two ounces of blood are sent out from the right and left ventricles. The heart beats about 72 times a minute. In half an hour, it is able to pump about 260 quarts of blood. Since there are only about six to seven quarts of blood in a full-grown man, the blood has to circulate through the body at a fairly fast rate.

The rate of the heartbeat is regulated by two sets of nerves. One makes the heart beat faster; the other slows it down. The nerve that makes the heart beat faster is called the accelerator nerve. The nerve that slows it down is called the vagus nerve. But we cannot change the rate of our heartbeat by deciding to do so. This is because the accelerator and vagus nerves are controlled by a part of the nervous system that works automatically. The heart, however, can beat independently of the nerves. The nerves simply change the speed of the heartbeat to conform to the body's requirements.

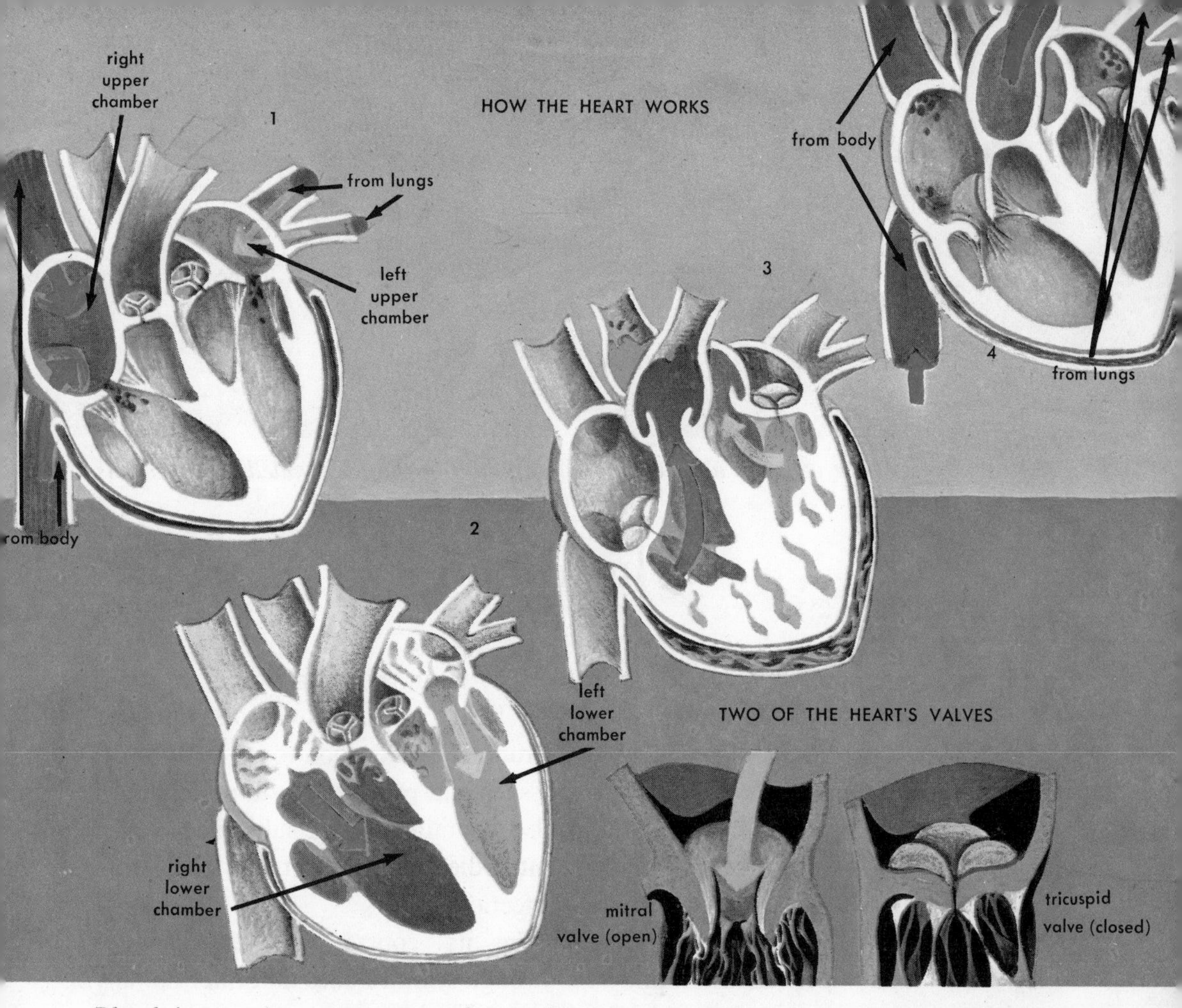

Blood from veins enters upper heart chambers (auricles). The auricles contract and force blood into lower chambers (ventricles). Ventricles contract, close valves from auricles, and open valves to arteries. Blood from the right ventricle is pumped through arteries to the lungs; blood from the left ventricle goes into artery that supplies body.

The heartbeat has three parts. The first part is the squeeze, the second part is the relaxation, and the third part is a period of rest. The period of rest is much shorter than the other two parts put together. When your heart beats fast, it is only the rest period that is shortened, not the time for the strokes.

The most wonderful thing about the heart is that it goes on beating throughout life, resting only a fraction of a second after each beat. Since this involves over 100,000 beats per day, the durability of this organ is obviously great.

Doctors once thought that the heart was an organ that could not be operated on. In recent years, however, surgeons have operated on more and more people with afflicted hearts, and they have often been able to make them strong and healthy.

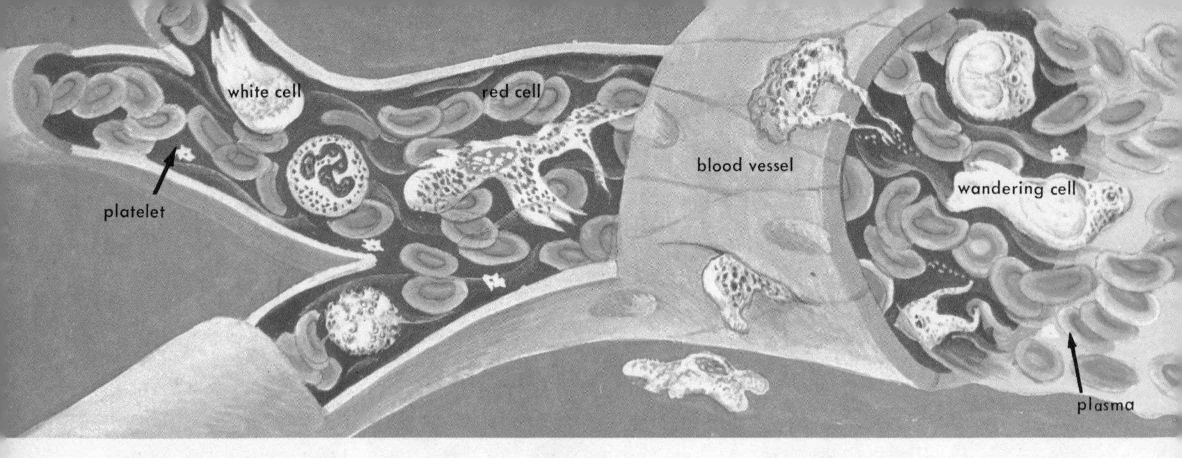

The wandering white cells are able to pass into and out of the thin-walled blood vessels.

The Blood

The blood is actually not a red fluid at all. An eye that could see the tiny things of the world would find that blood is a clear, pale yellow liquid, almost like water. Floating in it are great numbers of flat, round, red cells. A closer look would find other cells that are harder to see at first because they are the same watery color as the liquid in which they float. Some of these white cells have no regular shape. They move about by changing their shape.

In the human body there are more than 500 times as many red cells as there are white ones; and the number of red cells in a healthy person is about twenty trillion.

The blood circulates through the entire body. Each of the three main parts of the blood–the red cells, the white cells, and the clear yellow fluid–has its special job. Together they feed, supply, and even defend the cells of tissue that make up the human body.

The clear yellowish liquid, which is the fluid part of the blood, is called serum. It carries food to the cells of the tissues and removes waste materials. It also contains special substances called antibodies that protect the body from infection.

In its course, the fluid passes through lymph nodes that filter out any harmful substances–such as bacteria–that may have been collected.

The lymph and veins first receive food material from the hairlike villi of the small intestine. Fats are absorbed into the lymph vessels; amino acids and glucose into the veins. In general, the job of taking food materials to the various parts of the body is done by the blood.

The blood also delivers oxygen to the tissue cells. It has its special carriers, red cells, to deliver oxygen.

Red cells get their color from hemoglobin, a protein that contains iron.

The cells pick up oxygen from the air sacs in the lungs and carry it to the tissues in their hemoglobin. There the oxygen is released, goes into the plasma of the blood, and is carried directly to the tissues. Carbon dioxide is simultaneously picked up by the blood.

When the blood has picked up carbon dioxide, it returns to the lungs where it gives up this waste gas to the air in the air sacs. The gas is then exhaled. In the lungs, the red cells, which have lost their oxygen to the tissues, pick up a new load to distribute throughout the body.

The job of the white cells in the bloodstream is to protect the body against foreign substances such as bacteria. Certain white cells, because they have no regular shape, can smother enemy particles by flowing around them. When the enemy particle is inside the white cell, it is dissolved in special fluids which the white cell gives off.

When the body is infected by swarms of enemy bacteria, the number of white cells in the blood is increased, as if extra troops were being called out.

Red blood cells are manufactured in the marrow of the bones. Many white cells originate in the lymph nodes.

For many years, men looked for a way to replace lost blood with blood from a healthy person. Everyone who tried failed until scientists found that there were four different types of blood. Today, in the process called transfusion, blood can be given from one person to another, if both have the same or compatible types of blood.

If two different types of blood are mixed, the red cells clump together with dangerous results. To test whether two bloods are of the same type, the serum of one blood is added to cells from the other. If the red cells don't form clumps then the two bloods are of the same type or are compatible.

This diagram shows the four main types of blood and which ones will mix with which others. The solid red clump means that the two will mix, the dotted red means they will not.

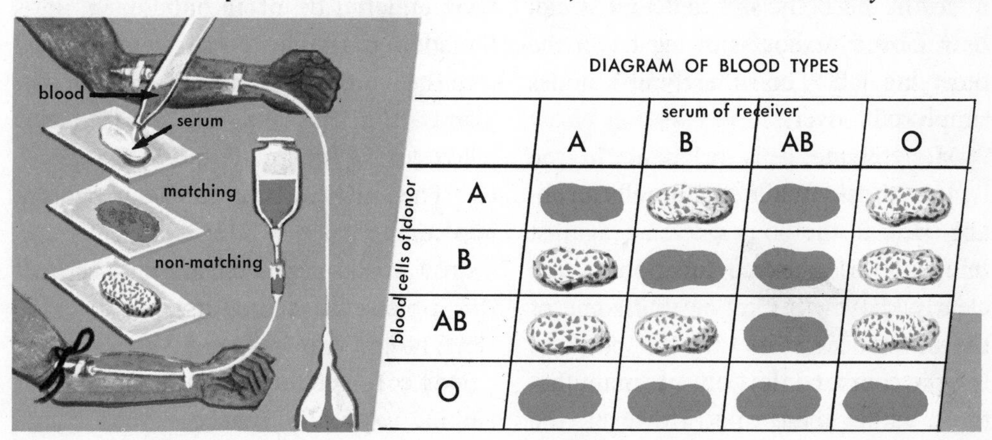

The Lymph System

The fluid that cells live in is the lymph fluid. It is salty, and contains the same salts that are found in the sea, except in smaller amounts.

The lymph fluid is part of the whole blood that has flowed out of the blood vessels, leaving the red blood cells behind. The lymph therefore has a watery color. It bathes the individual cells, feeding them with the nourishing substances that came from the small intestine.

Lymph flows from the spaces within the tissues into the lymph vessels and passes through progressively larger vessels into the veins. On the way, it filters through little balls of cells called lymph nodes.

These nodes act as cleansing stations where the bacteria and waste products from the cells are removed. For example, tonsils are lymph nodes; but since there are plenty of other lymph nodes in the body, infected tonsils can be removed without slowing down the purifying job. The other lymph nodes simply take over.

Many white cells originate in the lymph nodes. While these cells probably help in the body's defense against infection, their exact function is not clearly known. It may be that some of the substances made by the body to help it combat infection are manufactured within these cells. However, the cells do not move to the place where the infection is and engulf bacteria, as many other white cells do.

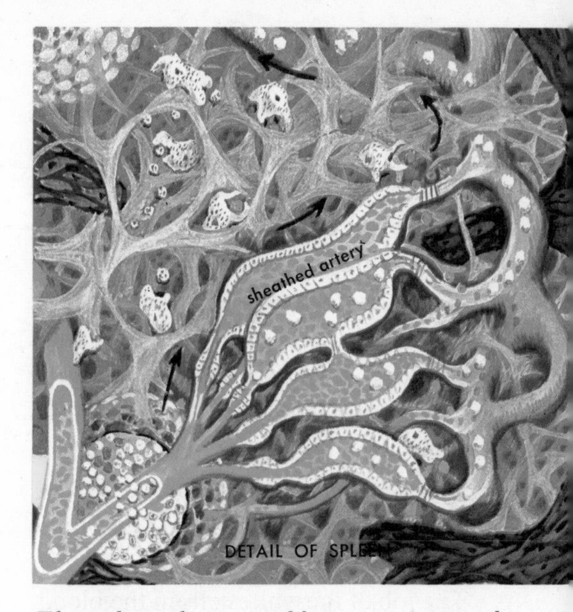

The spleen destroys old or worn-out red blood cells and acts as a reservoir for blood to be used in emergencies.

One of the most interesting parts of the lymph system is the spleen. This organ, a little smaller than a clenched fist, lies next to the stomach in the upper left side of the abdomen. It is made up of clusters of white blood cells, like those found in lymph nodes, and of spaces through which blood flows.

The chief functions of the spleen are to manufacture white blood cells, destroy worn-out red blood cells, and act as a blood storage reservoir.

The number of lymph vessels in the body is far greater than the number of blood vessels.

The Excretory System

The excretory system has the job of eliminating waste products from the body. It does this in four separate ways: through the skin, the lungs, the intestines, and the kidneys.

The skin eliminates sweat, which is 99% water, and sebum, the oily product of the glands connected to the hair root. The main purpose of the sweat glands, however, is to regulate the body temperature.

The lungs secrete carbon dioxide and water.

The intestine eliminates the remains of undigested food, bile salts, bacteria, and other waste products.

The body's blood purification system is centered in the kidneys. The blood that brings food and oxygen to the cells also carries away the wastes. To keep the amount of wastes in the body as low as possible, they must be removed as fast as they are formed. The cleansing of the blood is so important that the body has a special set of organs for this purification.

The body's cleansing organs are the kidneys. Each one has more than a million tiny filters. Blood is pumped forcefully to the kidneys from the

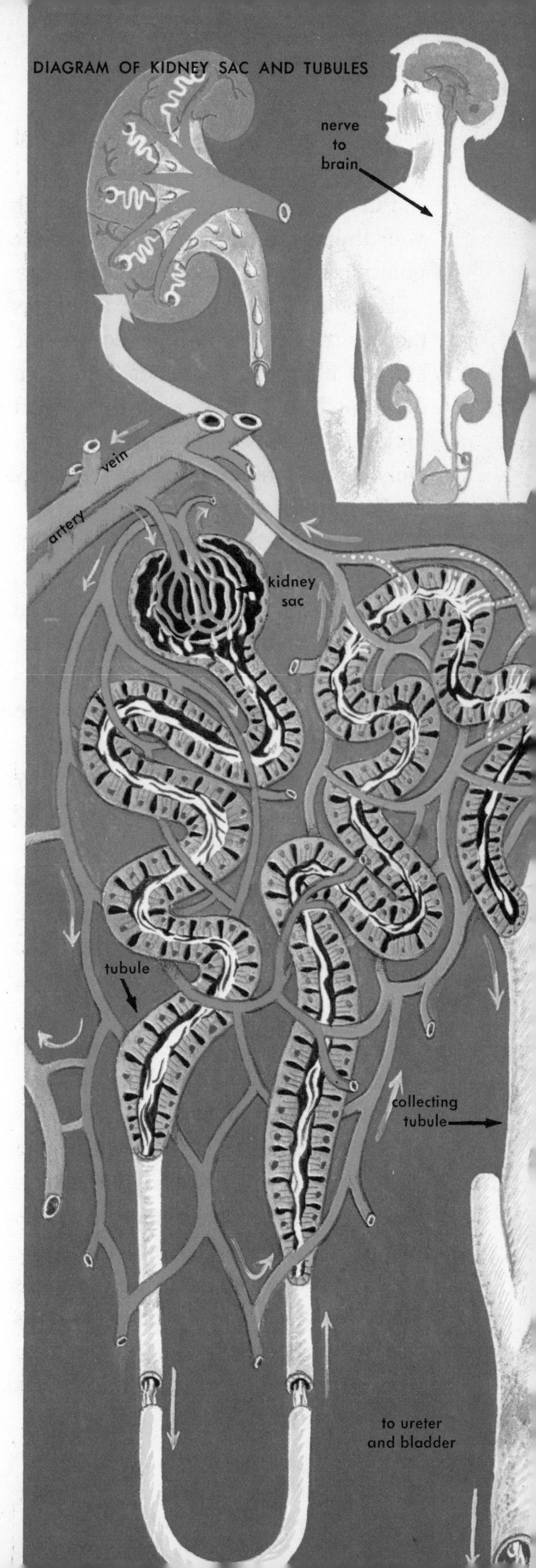

Wastes drain through tubules to bladder. A nerve tells brain when bladder is full.

heart, and in this way the bloodstream is cleansed under pressure.

Put your hands on your hips with your thumbs in back. Your thumbs are pointing to the lower ends of the kidneys.

Together, the kidneys are as big as the heart. In twenty-four hours, the kidneys filter 170 quarts of fluid from the blood, but they return the vast majority of this fluid to the blood. Only a small fraction leaves the body in the form of urine.

Each kidney is shaped like a bean. The outer portion is called the cortex; the inner part is the medulla. The medulla is made up of triangular sections called pyramids. These are pointed toward a glovelike sac called the pelvis, into which urine is secreted.

Kidneys contain millions of tiny blood vessels which are twisted into little coils. Each coil is almost completely surrounded by a double-layered sac the size of a pinpoint. The sacs are filters. Wastes are strained through the walls of the blood vessels into the sacs, which lead to tiny tubes called tubules. The tubules collect the waste and drain it off.

The millions of tiny blood vessels and filter systems from which the wastes are strained are in the cortex. Most of the draining tubules lie in the medulla. They point toward the pyramids, and join much as tiny streams come together to form larger streams that in turn join with other streams to form a river. The clusters of tubules end at the point of each pyramid. There the waste liquids pour into the kidney pelvis.

The liquid wastes that are collected in each kidney are then piped away through a long, hollow tube, the ureter. There is one ureter for each kidney. The ureters are about the size of a macaroni strand. Through the ureters the wastes reach a reservoir called the bladder. The bladder is like a bag. When it is empty, it is flat. When it is full, it is round and projects upward. At the lower end of the bladder is the urethra, through which urine passes out of the body.

Urine enters the bladder a little at a time, and the bag, which has a wall of muscle tissue, slowly fills up. When about a cupful is collected, nerves send messages to the brain. The brain knows that soon the urine will have to be sent out of the body. At the proper time and place, the brain signals to the muscles that control the urethra. A muscular ring around this tube relaxes. The bladder muscle presses down and the accumulated waste liquid is forced out.

When the urinary passage is clogged in one way or another, so that the waste liquids cannot escape freely, a pressure is built up. If this pressure gets too high, the passage of wastes from the blood into the tubules is held up. This causes an accumulation of waste in the bloodstream, and may be a symptom of any of several disorders.

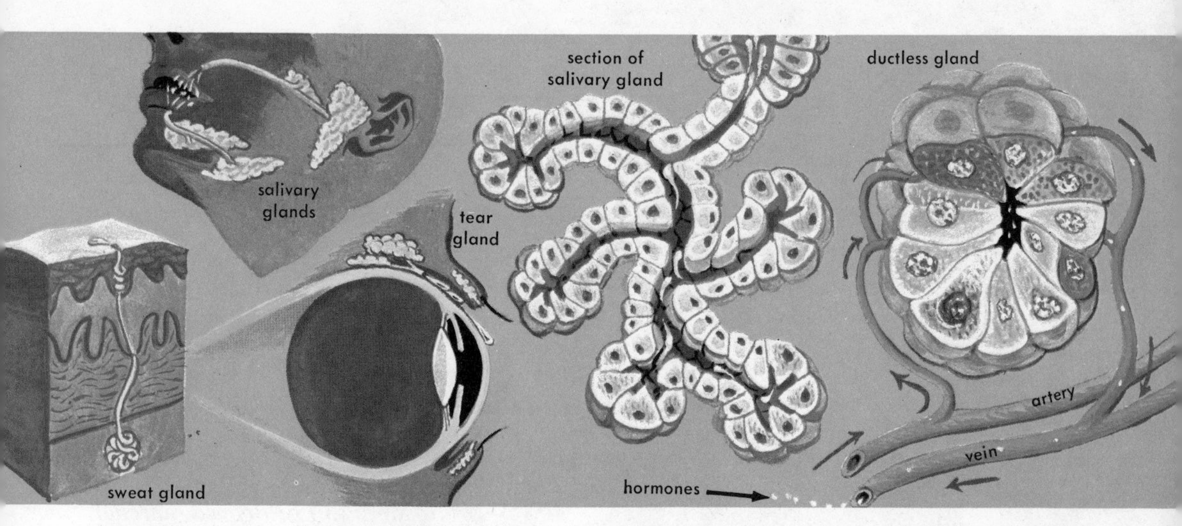

Some glands pour their fluids into the body through tiny openings. The endocrine, or ductless, glands, have no such openings. They supply hormones directly into the bloodstream.

Masters of the Body

Most glands are tiny sacs or tubes that manufacture special fluids which are poured through tiny hollow pipes called ducts. The glands that make hormones are different from these. They pour their fluids directly into the bloodstream. For this reason they are called the ductless glands. They are scattered throughout the body and they make up a special control system—the endocrine system. The hormones are the masters of the body.

The commander-in-chief of the ductless glands is the pituitary. The front and back parts of this gland are really two separate glands that are very close together.

The front part manufactures at least six different hormones. Five of these are special messengers that control other ductless glands, making this part of the pituitary the master gland of the entire system. The sixth hormone goes directly to the billions of body cells and directly controls their growth. It is called the growth hormone.

A hormone from the rear portion of the pituitary increases the blood pressure. It also tightens the muscles of the intestine, and decreases the secretion of urine.

One of the hormones from the front part of the pituitary, ACTH, is a special messenger controlling the adrenal glands.

Each adrenal gland is divided into an outer part, or cortex, and an inner part, or medulla.

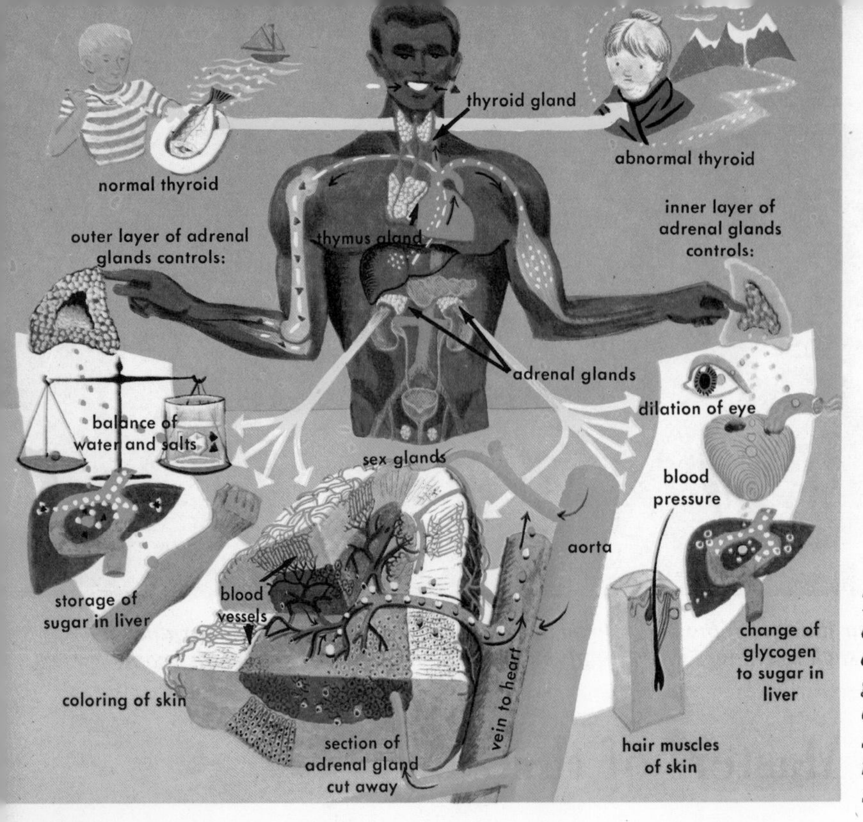

The thyroid, adrenal, and thymus glands are all ductless glands. The functions and the complicated structure of the adrenal glands are shown here.

The hormones of the cortex regulate the use and storage of protein, fat, and carbohydrate. They control the amount of water the body retains or excretes. They watch over the important salts of the body and influence growth.

The medulla secretes two hormones, of which the better known is adrenaline. It raises the blood pressure, increases the heart's activity and body temperature, and makes more sugar immediately available for use. In an emergency, the adrenal medulla prepares the body for flight or fight, depending upon what the brain decides to do. The other hormone of the medulla, called noradrenaline, is similar in structure and action to adrenaline.

A hormone from the front part of the pituitary controls the activity of the thyroid gland. The thyroid secretes a hormone that helps control the speed at which body cells work.

Behind the thyroid are four very much smaller glands, the parathyroids. They control the speed at which calcium is taken from the bones and deposited in the bloodstream, where it is important to the proper functioning of the nervous system.

Another hormone center in the pancreas directly controls the body's ability to use sugar. The hormone manufactured is called insulin. It passes through the bloodstream to the liver and muscles and allows them to take sugar from the blood and store it away in the form known as glycogen.

Reproduction

The reproduction of the entire living body starts from a combination of two cells which are different in shape, size, and–most particularly–origin. One comes from the male body; the other is made within the female.

The female cell, or ovum (the Latin word for egg), is produced about every twenty-eight days within the female body. It is about the size of a pinpoint, and disappears within a few days unless it is joined by a male cell.

The male cells also have an ancient name–sperm, from the Greek word for seed. The sperm cells are different from every other cell in the body. They are the only cells that can propel themselves about.

If sperm cells are present in the female body during the few days of an ovum's existence, one is likely to come in contact with the ovum. When this happens, the sperm enters the ovum. This is how a human being begins.

Even though the sperm and ovum look different, each contains a twisted pack of separate threadlike chains of

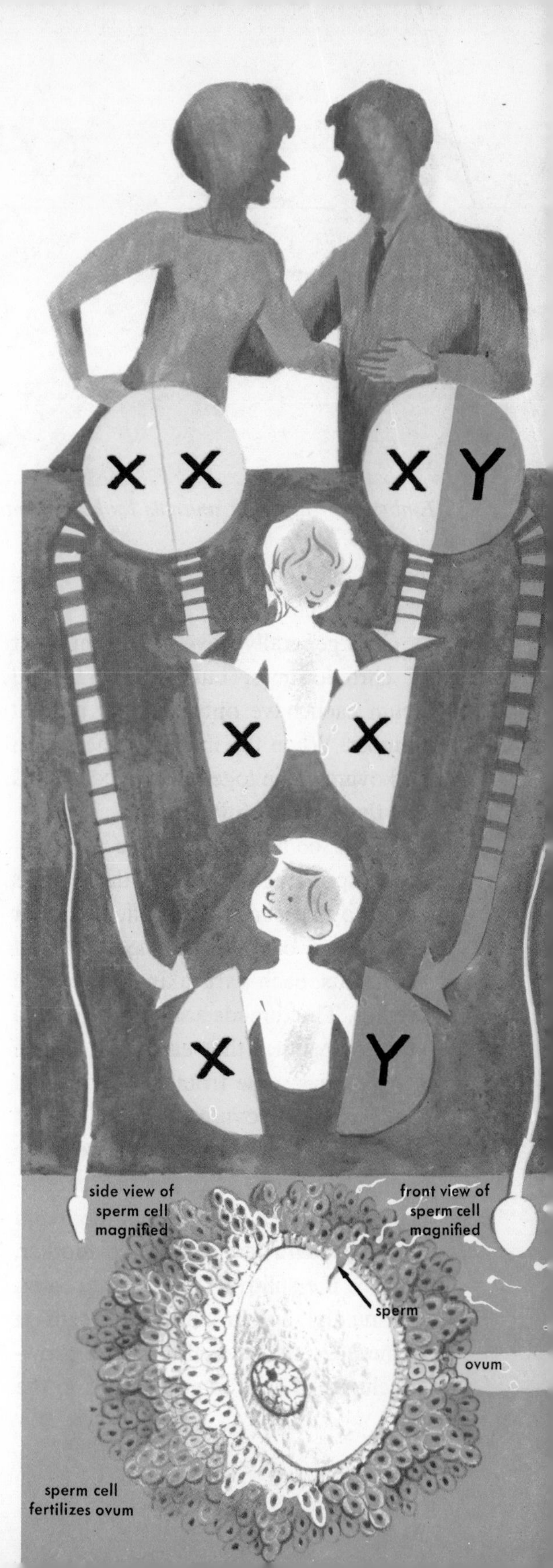

A child's sex is determined by chromosomes transmitted by the parents. There are two types of these chromosomes, called X and Y. Women have only X chromosomes; men have both X and Y. A child who receives two X-type chromosomes becomes a girl. One who receives an X and Y becomes a boy. Chromosomes are carried by ovum and sperm cells.

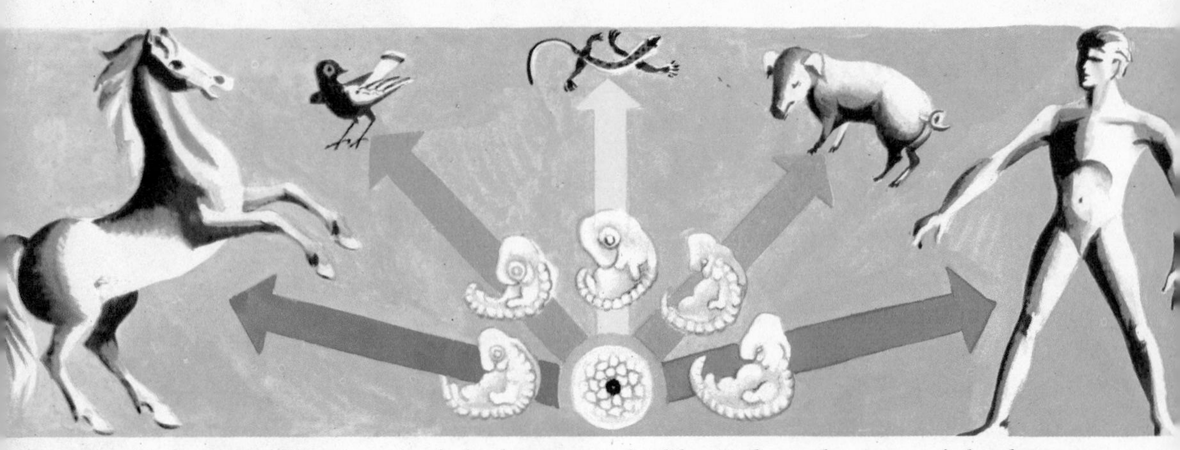

Embryos of different animals look very much alike in the early stages of development.

beads, or genes. The chains are called chromosomes.

Cells generally have a fixed number of chromosomes, but the sperm and ovum each have only half the normal number. When the nuclei of the sperm and ovum come together, the combined cell thus has the full amount.

In the combined cell, the chromosomes split lengthwise, half the threads going to one end of the cell, the other half to the other end. The cell itself then splits, each part taking half of the threads. The threads are by this time so tangled together that each part of the new cell has some from the sperm and some from the ovum. The genes that the sperm chromosomes carry are those that give the offspring the characteristics of the father. Those from the ovum give the characteristics of the mother.

Once the splitting begins, it goes on continually, and a cluster of cells is formed. On the seventh day, the growing cluster of cells attaches itself to the inner wall of the part of the mother's body called the uterus. The cluster of cells is eventually fed by blood passing through this point of attachment.

By the end of only three weeks, the single cell has grown into a many-celled being with a rounded shape and an extension of the body where the heart is already forming. As the days pass little buds appear which will grow to become arms and legs. The eyes begin to develop, and then the ears.

In the human embryo, as it is called, about two months old, a human form can already be recognized. Eyelids, nose, lips, ears, and cheeks can all be seen and the limb buds have taken on the appearance of arms and legs.

Between the third and fourth month, the size of the embryo doubles. The muscles have become active. The heartbeat is strong, having started about the fourth week. At the end of about another month, little toenails and fingernails have come into being. There

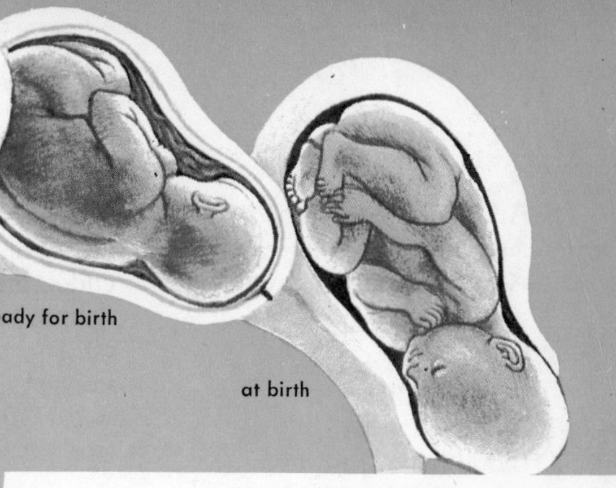

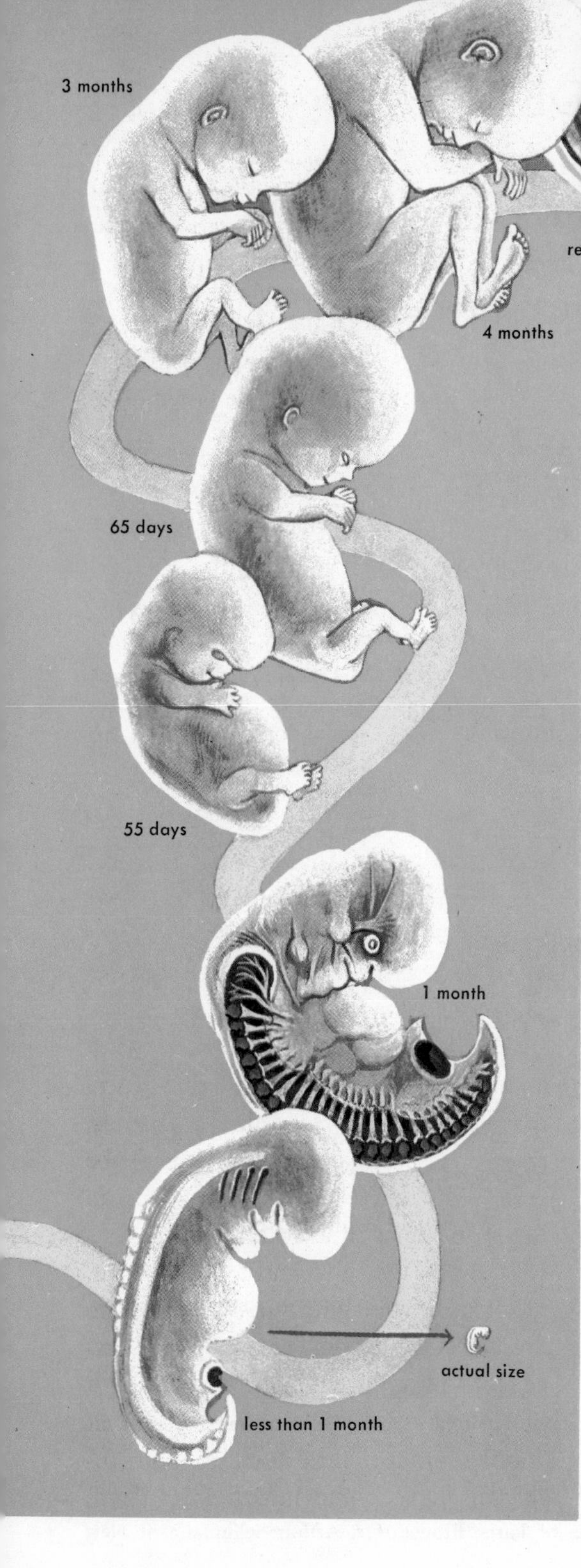

3 months

ready for birth

4 months

at birth

65 days

55 days

1 month

actual size

less than 1 month

is also the beginning of hair on the head.

However, many of the parts of the body necessary to life—such as those for breathing and digestion—are still not developed. They are still not ready to work even six months after the sperm and the ovum came together. The embryo's bloodstream is nourished by that of the mother through a special structure called the placenta, which is attached to the mother's uterus.

One month before the child is born, it weighs a few pounds and is around fifteen inches long. Whether it is to be a boy or girl has been clear for about five months now—ever since the end of the fourth month.

The last month before birth the length does not change very much but the weight increases greatly. The skin smooths out. The internal organs—circulation of blood, breathing, and digestion—are now fully developed. Finally, the baby is ready for the adventure of life in the outside world.

After the first three months or so, the human embryo is a miniature human being.

INDEX

The publishers gratefully acknowledge the cooperation of Alfred A. Knopf, Inc. in making available Fritz Kahn's *Man in Structure and Function* (1943), on which the idea and conception of many of the illustrations are based.

The artist also extends his sincere thanks to the following for their advice and assistance in preparing the illustrations for this book: Dr. M. Diesnis of Nice, France; Prof. Ovidio Lefebvre d'Ovidio of Rome, Italy, and São Paulo, Brazil; Dr. I. Knittel of Paris, France; Dr. Arthur Seligmann of New York City.